Beyond the Marathon:

The Grand Slam of Trail Ultrarunning

To James —
Good luck with
your trail ultrarunning!

Bob Boeder

June 29, 2022

Silverton, CO

Beyond the Marathon:

The Grand Slam of Train Ultrarunning

Robert B. Boeder

ISBN: 1-4752-8803-4
ISBN-13: 9781475288032

CONTENTS

Prologue

I can't stop sobbing. Every time I think I have a grip on myself my body is wracked by a new wave of uncontrollable blubbering. All the long lonely hours on the roads and trails, all the sweat and hard work of training, all the blisters, sore feet, aching legs, the expense of flying all over the country to these four races - it has all come down to this. My resolve to become one of the handful of ultrarunners to complete the Grand Slam is dissolving in a puddle of tears.

My breakdown comes at Lambs Canyon aid station, the 50-mile point of the Wasatch Front 100 Mile Endurance Run. I am 350 miles into my Grand Slam summer. All the stress of trying to finish four 100 mile trail races in the space of 14 weeks has come crashing down on me, like an avalanche in this rugged western sentinel of the Rocky Mountains.

Lambs Canyon aid station is curiously located at an underpass of I-80, the main highway entering Salt Lake City from the east. Aid stations are usually stuck in the middle of nowhere. The interstate follows Parley's Canyon, and I have been running on a trail alongside Parley's Creek. At Lambs Canyon, huge double trailer rigs hurtle by overhead as I bury my face in my arms and howl.

I've been running 14 hours, since 5:00 AM. The race course follows trails along the tops and sides of ridges above 8,000 feet. Every so often a canyon cuts into the mountainside. The canyons act like wind tunnels sucking air up from the valley of the Great Salt Lake far below. All day long I have been fighting 40-60 mile per hour winds on the ridge tops. The winds and the altitude are a double whammy, sucking fluids out of my body: I have lost 9 pounds, I'm severely dehydrated and I have stomach cramps and nausea. My dark green piss tells me I am in deep trouble: clear urine would mean I'm well hydrated and in good shape.

1

It's 7 PM. Phantoms wing through the dusk. The moon rises. Thunder and lightning rattle from the high passes. I know what awaits me in the darkness of the next 50 miles: Bear-Ass Pass, elevation 8,140 ft; Desolation Lake, 9,200 ft.; Red Lover's Ridge, 9,900 ft.; Scott's Pass, 9,460 ft; Catherine Pass, 10,480 ft.; Poleline Pass, 8,920; Point of Contention, 9,500 ft.

With all my experience why can't I do anything more productive than bawl my eyes out? I'm 52, I've been running for 20 years, and have competed in 250 races from 1 to 100 miles, including 8 triathlons, 34 marathons, and 31 ultras, 8 of them trail 100 milers. Perhaps my collapse is part of the quest, something I have to endure, like crossing a bridge of grief, in order to finish this race, complete the Grand Slam, and get on with the rest of my life.

My mind flashes back to December 1993 when I decided to take up the challenge of finishing these four most difficult 100 mile trail races in a single summer.

Chapter I

Training.

"Now bid me run,
And I will strive with things impossible;
Yea, get the better of them."

Julius Caesar, II, 1.324-6

On December 9, 1993, my adventure begins; planning for the Grand Slam summer commences and training gets serious. That's the day my Western States 100 Mile Endurance Run acceptance letter and 41 page *Participant's Guide* arrive in the mail from Race Directors Norm and Helen Klein.

"Congratulations!!!", the acceptance letter trumpets, "You have just become the winner of a 100 mile trip across the Sierra, from Squaw Valley to Auburn, California. Unfortunately, you will not be traveling by road nor rail, nor by plane nor train, but alas, you will be required to make this spectacular journey on foot."

Western States, held on the last weekend in June, is the second race in the Grand Slam series. The other events are: the Old Dominion 100 Miler staged in Fort Valley, Virginia, the first weekend in June; the Leadville Trail 100 Mile Endurance Run which takes place in the Colorado Rockies the third weekend in August; and Utah's Wasatch Front 100 Mile Endurance Run in early September. The Vermont 100 Mile Endurance Run held on the last weekend in July in Woodstock, Vermont, can be substituted for Old Dominion, but the other three races are obligatory. Each event is more difficult than the preceding one due to increasing altitude, the terrain becoming more severe, and the growing exhaustion of the runner.

Section VII of the *Participant's Guide*, "Medical and Other Risk Factors", endorses Western States as, "one of the most physically taxing events in the world." A partial list of the risks I have signed up for includes renal shutdown, heat stroke, injuries from falling, snow hazards, effects of cold/hypothermia, wildlife hazards, vehicle hazards, risks associated with low sodium and chloride counts, altitude sickness, and muscle necrosis.

Necrosis? I have to look it up: "The pathological death of living tissue in a plant or animal." Great.

The risk list continues: overuse injuries, common fatigue, poison oak, difficulty in gaining access to or locating injured participants, and getting lost. One particular sentence catches my eye. "Please note that death can result from several of the risk conditions discussed below, or from other aspects of participation in the Western States Run."

Not everyone who pays $145 and submits proof of qualification by completing a 50- or 100-mile race is allowed to challenge death in the high mountain heat and dust of California. Elite trail runners are assured of entry, but Western States has a lottery for duffers like me. This is the third successive year I have won the privilege of courting martyrdom in the High Sierras. I'm just lucky, I guess.

Entry into Western States used to be more difficult. In the late 1980s, over 1000 runners applied each November for the 425 places in the race, so a lottery was introduced to select the field of participants. The drawing is held in Auburn, California, and is open to the public. Losers have been known to leave town in tears.

One little known sports fact is that in the early 1990s the number of 100-mile trail races proliferated from four to a dozen. This growth means fewer people are fighting to get into Western States, so I assume that is why I have lucked out for three years in a row.

It's not because I am a top dog or even a threat to come in under 24 hours, the goal of the better trail runners. In 1993, I finished 202 out of 209, my time of 29:46 was only 14 minutes under the 30 hour cutoff.

Receiving my acceptance into the Western States race is exciting, but I'm getting ahead of myself. The story of 400 miles of trail running starts with the basic elements that constitute the sport of endurance running.

First, what exactly is trail ultrarunning? At the 1990 Wasatch Front 100 Mile awards ceremony a runner named Neil Beidleman noted, "This is a sick sport."

Neil's statement reflected his state of mind upon completing one of the toughest running events in the world. Californian John Demorest is more upbeat. He calls trail running an opportunity to hang around "a very special group of obsessive-compulsives who have a love for adventure and a spirit for fun."

Technically, any foot race that is not run primarily on pavement and is longer than the standard 26.2 mile marathon distance qualifies as a trail ultra. Most of the course should be on some kind of trail or dirt road, hopefully in a scenic setting. It's also a sport where paramedics are waiting for the participants every 5-10 miles.

World 50-mile record holder (4:50:21), South African, Bruce Fordyce, expresses his attitude toward the sport simply: "Running," he says, "gives a man a glimpse of the greatest freedom he can ever know. It liberates the body and the mind."

Veteran ultrarunner and naturalist, Bernd Heinrich, takes a more intellectual approach: he says, "I came to be attracted to running because it is an individual sport that is 'pure' - hard, elegant, exact. It is performed at its purest, judged by the watch and the tape, totally unadulterated (and hopefully unadulterable) by anyone's personal judgments or interpretations."

For me, ultrarunning is a passion, a state of mind, a fierce avocation. It's also a journey into the darkest recesses of the mind and body, one of the few opportunities available to the average person to explore his physical, mental, emotional and spiritual limits.

Why do I run ultras? Involvement in ultra running constitutes a vital part of my life. Entering the events gives me goals, something to look forward to; the long-distance training keeps me at a high level of fitness and introduces me to people who share similar interests and who become my best friends.

I admit that I am addicted to long distance running. I aim to run 7 days a week, 52 weeks a year. On the rare day when I'm unable to run my body doesn't feel right. It doesn't matter where I am or what I'm supposed to be doing. I make time to run, in every type of weather and in every kind of location. I don't care about awards or t-shirts. I don't suffer from bucklemania — a word coined by ultrarunners to describe the overwhelming urge to run 100 miles in under 24 hours in order to win a belt buckle. It's the effort that counts.

All my activities revolve around the sport. If I can't fit a run into an outing or a vacation then I don't go. I crave running like a junkie craves his fix, like an alcoholic needs his booze. I'm not exaggerating. I know about addiction because I am a recovering alcoholic and drug abuser.

Between ages 15 and 40, I was drunk nearly every night. For 17 of those 25 years I used drugs. For recovering substance abusers, the question of what to do with all the time they previously devoted to getting high is a serious issue. For me, the answer was easy. I would run more. I started running in my early 30's when I was still drinking and smoking dope because one day when I looked in the mirror, I saw a flabby, jowly, unhappy guy. I decided to change that image by getting in shape.

My decision came in the mid-1970s, at the beginning of the running boom when Bill Rodgers and Frank Shorter were American sports heroes. So I started running short distances, eventually working up to a mile a day. I liked it. My only previous running experience was trying to be a hurdler on my high school track team for one year, but even at 15 I was already out of shape, smoking cigarettes and drinking beer, hellbent on self-destruction.

By 30 I had quit smoking tobacco, but I continued to smoke marijuana, which I found to be the less destructive of the two substances. Running became a daily ritual, but I was going through a non-competitive, semi-hippy phase of my life, so I didn't enter any races. Sometimes I ran after smoking a joint or having a couple of beers. I didn't see anything strange about this behavior. I convinced myself that my ability to run 1 or 2 miles easily proved that I didn't have a problem with alcohol.

But drinking certainly was a compulsion. People who don't have that addictive gene in their bodies cannot imagine what it is like to have something inside driving them toward that next drink or that next fix. To an addict, excess is best. Nothing can stop the desperate need to get high, a need which dictates how every second of one's life is spent. An addict can lose his job, his family, his belongings, and come close to losing his life and still insist, stubbornly and singlemindedly, on having one more drink, one more hit.

Eventually, when I was 40, I voluntarily stopped doing drugs. Something bad seemed to happen every time I smoked a reefer or snorted coke. I was getting low instead of high. Saying goodbye to alcohol was harder. Generally, a drunk won't face up to his problem until he hits bottom. In September 1982, my family and I were living in a dilapidated house in an unincorporated Florida swamptown. I was unemployed, drunk by 10 AM every day, angry all the time, avoided by my kids. One morning, following another night of self-inflicted misery, I woke up to discover my wife loading our three children into a vehicle and driving away. That was my bottom. I had had enough.

Six weeks in a treatment center followed, then years of weekly AA meetings, and, finally a divorce, but, through it all, faith, family and fitness have been my salvation. I retain my compulsive personality, but I have re-channeled the need to medicate myself with alcohol into an urge to run. For me, it's as if there were two parallel rail lines, the booze line and the run line. I was traveling on the booze line and the treatment center was a station on the line where I switched over to the run line. The booze line is still there, but it has become overgrown with weeds, and trains no longer use it. The run line is clean and fast, and trains skim over it effortlessly every day.

In the spring of 1983, I began entering 5K and 10K races; then, in October, after increasing my weekly mileage to 60 including a 15-20 mile training run every Saturday, I ran the Twin Cities Marathon, my first 26.2 miler. More marathons followed; then I discovered ultras through *UltraRunning* magazine, published in Sunderland, Massachusetts. Seeking a career as a free-lance writer, I had written an article about Bruce Fordyce, nine-time Comrades Marathon winner. Searching for a suitable publication for my manuscript, I found *UltraRunning*. The magazine editors offered no payment for my labors. Instead, they gave me a one year subscription.

Reading *UltraRunning* motivated me to try long-distance trail running, and in October, 1986, I finished my first trail ultra, the Mountain Masochist 50 Miler in the Blue Ridge Mountains near

Lynchburg, Virginia. 1986 was also the year the Grand Slam was born: Tom Green, a 35 year old house painter from Columbia, Maryland, became the first person to complete the big four trail races in a single summer.

On January 6, 1994, my Leadville entry form arrives in the mail. The race organizers are excited about this year's event because they have a new sponsor, Rockport Shoes, and the race will be filmed for television. I have to pay off my Christmas bills first, so I can't enter immediately, but my check for $145.00 is in the mail by the end of the month. Leadville is a popular race and fills its quota of 350 runners quickly.

On January 8, 1994, I finish the Charlotte Observer Marathon in 3:29 on a cool sunny morning. I feel good the entire race, but stiffen up in the last few miles due to the windy conditions. In 1987, I ran 3:09 at Charlotte to qualify for the Boston Marathon for the first time. 3:09 came as a complete shock to me. It just happened. I had no idea I could run that fast. Racing is like that. Sometimes a runner will have a good day and the result will surprise everyone, especially the runner.

Part of my success that day was due to being relaxed but ready to race. Endurance athletes, like musicians, are concerned about the psychological baggage they carry to the starting line of a race. They are aware that they have days when they can't "get loose," when their minds are clogged, their legs stiff. But like the musician, good day or bad, the athletes must perform. The trick is to relax enough to let the energy flow freely and the legs move naturally while remaining focused. Too much tension interferes with the smooth flow of physical response through muscles and nerves. Too little tension, as if the athlete is lying half asleep in a Jacuzzi, results in the early termination of the race.

Long distance runners must be alert, highly concentrated, attuned to the mechanics of their bodies, the terrain they are crossing, the ebb and flow of the race around them. Talent is necessary, but it isn't enough. The most successful, like the best musicians, work hard at their craft.

On January 15, 1994, my training program takes me to the Uwharrie National Forest near Troy, North, Carolina, to lope 20 miles in 5 hours. Every February I organize a three-in-one running event called the Uwharrie Trail Adventure Run on this tough hiking trail. Runners choose their distance — 8, 20, or 40 miles of trail twists and turns, rocks, sticks, roots, and fallen leaves. It's a hilly treacherous place, the site of several exhausted gold mines. Storm-uprooted trees occasionally block the path and runners negotiate numerous stream crossings. Training on the Uwharrie Trail a couple of times a month will be good preparation for the four summer 100 milers.

On February 12, a cool, overcast day, I run the Carolina Marathon in Columbia, South Carolina, in 3:23:30. After passing through the half way point in 1:40, I place seventy-first out of 250 finishers; second out of 23 in my 50-55 year old age group. I feel strong the entire distance. Not many years ago, running a standard 26.2 mile marathon was a major effort for me. Now I regard marathons as good training exercises.

On March 12, at the Catoctin Mountains 35 KM Trail Race near Frederick in northwestern Maryland, I finish in 5:51, 32nd of 73 starters and second in my age group. Two feet of snow blanket the trail. With the temperature in the 20's at the start, it is possible to run on top of the frozen snow crust until mid-day when the snow softens, causing my feet to sink in and slowing my progress considerably. Even so, I'm happy with my effort since I am able to run many uphill sections which I would walk normally in a longer race. Cross training on my Concept II Rowing Ergometer machine and Nordic Track machine is making me stronger and more agile on the trails.

Each evening I cross train for 20 minutes, alternating the two machines every other night. Occasionally, on weekends, I will row and Nordic Track on the same day. These exercises have been very effective in building overall muscle tone and especially in strengthening my quadriceps, abdominal, and lower back muscles, which are so important for uphill running.

I learned about the importance of upper body strength in ultra trail running through personal experience and by reading an interview with Helen Klein of Rancho Cordova, California, in *UltraRunning*. In 1988, during Helen's first attempt at the Grand Slam, when she was 65 years old, she was exhausted by the climbs at Old Dominion. She had to stop several times on the long uphills just to catch her breath. Bob Baska, the OD medical director, suggested that her problem was poor posture, not her lungs.

Specifically, she needed to strengthen the muscles that supported her shoulders and she also needed stronger abdominal muscles.

It was too late to start building those muscles for the '88 Slam, but Helen joined a health club that fall, spent the winter building up her upper body, and was among the first group of women to complete the Grand Slam in 1989. Helen has also been a proponent of the idea that the extreme stress of running ultras slows the aging process, both physically and mentally.

My time is 3:35 at the Ellerbe Springs Marathon on April 16, good for 15th overall out of 87 finishers, first in my age group. Ellerbe, North Carolina, is located 45 miles southwest of my home in Fayetteville. The course is hilly and rural. High humidity bothers some runners at the start of the race, but cloud cover and a fresh breeze keep conditions decent. I feel fine after the race and run ten miles the next day.

In early April, my Saturday training run increases to 27 miles and I go 10 on Sunday. This cranks up my mileage to over 70 per week. By early May I'm into the 80-miles-per-week zone. My final preparation for the Grand Slam summer calls for a 50-mile training run on the Old Dominion course on April 30, followed by Eric Clifton's Hurricane Ridge 50 KM race on the Blue Ridge Parkway in the mountains of Western North Carolina on May 14, three weeks before Old Dominion.

Training Encounter 1:

Seated at the backyard picnic table of Ronnie "Bubba" Bibb, my neighbor in Fayetteville, North Carolina, I am watching him chow down on a plateful of barbecue ribs, the traditional meal of choice around here. Ronnie is my height, 6 feet tall, but weighs 340 pounds, nearly twice as much as I do. He shouts at his wife, Sharhonda, "Hey, Shug, get Bob a mess of ribs before he dies of hunger." Ronnie and Sharhonda form a reverse North Carolina version of Jack Spratt and his wife with Ronnie the fat eater and his wife the skinny chain smoker.

I decline Ronnie's offer. "Too much fat, Bubba" I inform him: "I only eat a small piece of lean meat once a day — usually fish or chicken." If I tell Ronnie that the rest of my low fat, low salt diet consists mainly of carbohydrates — fruits and fruit juices, vegetables, nuts, bread, yoghurt, bagels, and various vitamin and mineral supplements - vitamin E, zinc, extra iron, and a daily multi-vitamin pill — he'll call me a communist, so I spare him the details.

"So what're you fixin to do this summer, Bob?" Ronnie asks.

"I'm going to run a hundred mile race," I reply.

Ronnie's brow furrows and his eyes bulge out. I have a moment of panic. Ronnie seems to be choking as barbecue juice dribbles down his chin and drips onto his overalls, but he recovers in time to suck the meat off another rib.

"Say what? You're gonna run a hunnerd miles? Why I wouldn't drive a hunnerd miles, much less run that far. What's gotten into you, Bob? You used to be a right sensible feller. Hey Shug, get Bob some hush puppies. He's gonna need some energy."

I don't have the courage to tell Ronnie that I am "fixin" to run not only one but four 100-mile trail races this summer. I don't want to send him into lunchtime convulsions.

I don't really expect Bubba to understand. Basically, I'm alone in this endeavor. No one but me is convinced I can finish the Grand Slam. My family thinks I am foolish to try. Even my closest trail running pals are not wildly enthusiastic about my chances.

In this part of North Carolina, endurance trail runners are as scarce as kangaroos. Fayetteville is football country. Being the home of Fort Bragg and the 82nd Airborne Division, it is one of the least politically correct towns in the entire USA, a place where the most popular bumper sticker reads, "My kid beat up your honor student."

Fayetteville has more tatooed women per 1000 inhabitants than anywhere in the country except maybe Los Angeles and Fayetteville is also the Fat Capitol of the Western Hemisphere. The "Eat Healthy" revolution hasn't reached our neck of the woods yet. As far as my neighbors are concerned, butter, bacon grease, Budweiser, and Moon Pies are the four main food groups.

Ronnie does have a point. What has gotten into me?

I'm not sure. Midlife crisis, maybe. I'm 51 years old — middle aged chronologically — although I feel youthful and am physically stronger than I have ever been. Looking for a challenge, perhaps. At 51 I can't win a 10K race outright, but if I train hard enough I can outlast most runners half my age. The question keeps coming up. Why submit to this self-flagellation? The answers seem lame: Because it's fun; I enjoy it immensely; it's the most exciting idea

I've ever had. One thing is certain: to enter a 100 mile trail race, you have to have a dream, a want, or a void. It's not for everyone.

On April 24, heat training starts on my first really miserable, long (20 miles), lonely, hot (80 — 90 degrees) training run on Longstreet at Fort Bragg. I carry three 20-ounce water bottles with me to fight off dehydration during the 3 hour training run. I have lots more of these runs to look forward to during the next 4-5 weeks leading up to OD.

Another sign of the commencement of serious training is my switch from a nightly heaping, fat-filled bowlful of Death by Chocolate ice cream to no-fat sherbet — still in large quantities. Maybe the diet change plus running in the heat will slim me down from my present 175 pounds to 165. I also mail my $100 entry fee to the Old Dominion race management. I'm holding off on entering Wasatch until I see what happens at Old Dominion and Western States.

In previous years I completed Old Dominion, Leadville, and Vermont (in my 100 mile personal best time of 22:21) once each, and Western States twice, but I have never set foot on the Wasatch Front course. This lack of direct knowledge of the final Grand Slam test is scary. Invariably, every article I read comparing the Big Four 100 mile events rates the Utah race as the most difficult. Throughout the summer Wasatch lurks in the background like a 10 ton boulder teetering on the edge of a cliff poised to tumble down squashing my hopes and dreams.

By the end of April, I am well satisfied with my training. I have been injury free all spring, and I'm not suffering from the nagging muscle soreness in my groin and at the points where my hamstrings connect with my pelvis that have bothered me in the past. I credit cross training on my rowing and Nordic Track machines for strengthening these muscles.

On April 30, a 50-mile training run at Fort Valley, Virginia, takes me 11-1/2 hours to complete. Nine of us gather at Pat Botts' farm in Fort Valley for the 7 AM start. Pat is the founder of the Old Dominion race and the best female grand master (over 50) 100-mile trail runner in the country. She consistently beats me and most other men in trail race competition.

The other runners are my Fayetteville training partners, Harvey Hall and Mike Robertson, Andy Peterson of Luray, Virginia, King

Jordan of Washington DC, Al Montgomery from Columbia, South Carolina, Chris Rodatz from Jacksonville, Florida and "Mr. Adonis", Rick Schneider from Abingdon, Maryland. It's a good group, sharing lots of bad jokes and poking fun at each other. These long training runs with friends are one of the best aspects of ultrarunning.

In the morning, the weather is warm and humid, but cloud cover prevents major heat buildup as the afternoon hours wear on. The course covers the middle miles of the Old Dominion race from Pat's house to Hechts Farm then ascends to the top of the Massanutten Mountain Ridge and Kennedy's Peak. We follow the dreaded Duncan Hollow trail, turn right on Chrisman Hollow Road, run the long uphill to Edinburg Gap, clamber along the rocky All Terrain Vehicle road and finally jog State Road 770 back to Pat's.

Shouting, "I'm a California man," signifying Western States, where the local runners specialize in scorching the downhills, I hammer the descents. Alternating running with speed walking, I feel comfortable the whole way except for the final two miles when my gas tank registers empty. I finish with a blister on the inside of my left foot, a sore left calf muscle, and a slightly swollen/reddened right ankle — all minor ailments that disappear overnight.

This training run on the Old Dominion course is just what I need. It focuses my attention on the early June race and gives me the confidence I need to handle raceday conditions.

My maiden attempt at running 100 miles was at Old Dominion in 1987. My brother, Bruce, crewed for me and joined me as a pacer for the last 25 miles. Crossing the Shenandoah River at the 82 mile point, we arrived at an unmarked intersection. A brief brotherly argument ensued, and — at dawn, 25 hours into the race — we turned right when we should have gone straight. After running 3 or 4 extra miles we found our way back to the course, but for me the mistake was psychologically devastating. At the 95 mile point, after 28 hours, I collapsed, physically and mentally. I could go no farther.

Totally exhausted, I was still proud of myself. I had given it everything I had. Ninety-five miles was farther than I had ever run before, and I learned a lot. The DNF (did not finish) was a monkey on my back, so I went back in 1988 and finished the race in 28:24. I had learned one of my early trail running lessons: if you want to race well on trails, you have to train on them.

Meteorological update: Runners are real weather hawks. Being outside so much we can come close to predicting the weather for every weekend of the year. This year, the last two weeks in April are hot in Fayetteville, but the first two weeks in May are unusually mild with temperatures in the 70's and low humidity — good running weather, but I'm not getting any heat training.

On May 14, I'm supposed to run Eric and Shelby Hayden-Clifton's Hurricane Ridge 50 Km race on the Blue Ridge Parkway near Laurel Springs, North Carolina. In 1992, after winning four 100-mile trail races, Eric was selected as national ultra runner of the year. He is the course record holder at Old Dominion (15:10) and Vermont (14:25). In 1991, Shelby was the top woman finisher at Old Dominion (21:32), and she is a champion endurance bike rider.

As it turns out, their "race" — actually a no T-shirt, no awards, no fee fun run — is cancelled after the parkway rangers refuse to issue a permit because running on parkway trails is, in their opinion, "too dangerous." This opinion is ridiculous — another "Write Your Congressman" issue for trail runners.

Instead of 50 km (31 miles), Dan Besse, of New Bern, North Carolina, Nancy and Rick Hamilton, Eric, Shelby, and I tackle 30 km (18.6 miles) on trails in the Greensboro, North Carolina, park system. Although I was looking forward to the 50 km, this is a stiff 3-1/2 hour workout which I run hard. The only negative consequence is a raging case of poison oak on my right elbow.

Training Encounter 2:

May 15 — the course is an 18 mile loop from my house to the small community of Rockfish, North Carolina, and back. The weather has finally warmed up. I feel tired even before I start. This training run quickly degenerates into a no-fun slog through eastern North Carolina, a land of pine trees, tobacco fields, and sandy soil. Fourteen miles into the workout, as I am chugging along the gravel shoulder of Stoney Point Road, a blue 1977 Chevrolet Monte Carlo with two women in it slows as it passes. One of the women leans out the passenger side window. In a voice redolent of stale cigarettes, cheap whiskey, and fragrant armpits, she yells, "Hey baby, I gotta burger if you gotta shake."

All the blood has drained from my brain into my feet. I am not quick thinking enough to holler an appropriate response, so all I can do is waggle my parched tongue at her as the Monte Carlo accelerates down the road towards Rockfish.

This fleeting encounter gives me food for thought for the remainder of the afternoon. What is the "burger" this woman referred to? Did she spot the love handles lurking underneath my running singlet? I'm fairly lean, so there isn't much else of me to "shake." Does sex play a role in ultrarunning?

People often ask what I think about during long runs. The truth is that when I am running alone, sex doesn't often intrude on my thoughts. It's too distracting. I do a lot of day dreaming. Sometimes my mind is a total blank. I use training runs to sort out personal and job-related matters, and I think about how my body feels, how my training is progressing, my next race, or in this case my next four races.

When ultra runners train or race in groups, I'll admit the stories we exchange can be in very poor taste and, yes, sex is one of the many topics we discuss.

Most of the time during a race I concentrate on the task at hand, where I am placing my feet, the time remaining, the weather, terrain, darkness, the messages my body is sending. It's like I am a computer operator monitoring a deep space probe listening intently for faint signals from within: "Your fluid level is low, Bob;" "A Coke would taste good now;" "Time for a Powerbar;" "Slow down, you're going to fast." If I heed these calls, I complete the race; if I don't, my body shuts down and I do not finish.

On May 21, I enter the Armed Forces Day 10K at Fort Bragg. My time is 42:04, good for third place in the 40-and-over age group. It feels like I'm going a lot faster than I am, thus revealing the wide gap between my perception of reality and what is actually happening. The course is hilly on a cool and windy day, and I beat most of the young soldiers entered in the race. The 10K is a good speed tuneup for Old Dominion. Afterward I run 16 miles on Longstreet to get in my miles for the day.

Those who write about ultramarathoning tend to dwell on the intense pain produced by running long distances. In an *Outside* magazine profile of Ann Trason, John Brant wrote, "The essence of ultrarunning is not so much avoiding pain and trouble as adjusting to their inevitable appearance."

15

I think that in this context, "pain" is the wrong word to use. During a race my feet "hurt" and my lungs "ache," but if a runner experiences excruciating pain, then something is broken and he should drop out of the race and have an x-ray of the painful area. Endurance cyclists, like the riders in the Tour de France, speak of "suffering" during their rides. That's the word I prefer to describe what I go through during a 100 miler. I suffer.

But suffering isn't necessarily a negative experience. As the Bible says, "We rejoice in our sufferings, knowing that suffering produces endurance, and endurance produces character, and character produces hope, and hope does not disappoint us, because God's love has been poured into our hearts...."

My upcoming ordeal divides into three parts: first, Old Dominion and Western States, three weeks apart; then a seven week break; finally, Leadville and Wasatch, also three weeks apart. I know what kind of effort it takes to run 100 miles. My main job will be to keep physically strong and motivated through the summer; to remain positive, upbeat, and focused on completing each race as it comes along. Staying injury free is crucial and will depend on luck and not doing anything stupid.

Being able to recover quickly is important for Grand Slammers. I'm thinking ahead about the importance of icing my feet and ankles immediately after each race to reduce swelling, of having a massage to reduce the soreness in my leg muscles by flushing out the lactic acid buildup, and of doctoring the inevitable blisters on my feet.

Sore feet are among the most common problems ultrarunners face. Feet are a neglected part of the human anatomy. Inside a foot are 26 bones, 3 arches, and innumerable ligaments and muscles. Feet take a terrible beating on hard surfaces, gravel roads, and rocky trails. To reduce blisters, veteran ultrarunners recommend buying running shoes a full size larger than normal and tying the laces loosely because feet swell during long races. Feet also get wet, which promotes blistering. During a race I don't change shoes or socks because it takes too much time and it seems that new shoes just promote blisters in different places on my feet, so why bother?

It's Sunday, May 22. I return to the 18 mile Rockfish loop. No sign of a Chevy Monte Carlo. Two weeks to go. I'm getting antsy.

Training Encounter 3:

It's hot. I'm waddling along Fisher Road, 3 miles from home, minding my own business, when I hear the sound every runner fears — barking dogs. Released from their chains, three medium-sized mongrels, brimming with pent-up aggression, spot me and immediately give chase. Turning to face them, I show my teeth in a menacing snarl.

The lead attacker is a mixed black lab. Stepping toward him with my right foot, I swing my size 12 left foot as hard as I can, catching him on the side of his head. This blow sends the canine tumbling into a ditch alongside the road.

Attacker number two appears to have had a doberman somewhere among his ancestors. Assessing the fate of his brother assailant, he calls off the assault and turns sharply onto Fisher Road where he is struck by a passing pickup truck.

Attacker number three, part of whose heritage includes a collie, calculates the cost of his kennelmates' foolhardy raid, and wisely decides to cancel this sortie: he turns tail and retreats without joining the battle.

For an ultrarunner, being chased by a pack of dogs is almost a compliment. At least the animals are showing some interest in an activity that attracts few spectators and fewer sponsors. Western States and Leadville have been televised, but trail running remains an amateur sport.

The minimal material rewards make trail running an egalitarian pastime where the egos of the top runners remain under control. The middle-and back-of-the-pack runners form the best audience for the elite athletes. Friendly, tolerant, and competent, the average ultrarunners know what is being put into a race, they approach their craft with humility, and they respect those who do it well.

May 30. Memorial Day. Sixteen miles in four hours on the Uwharrie Trail at a leisurely 15 minute per mile pace. A cool front has moved in. The temperature is in the high 70's with a breeze, the prettiest day I have ever spent in the Uwharrie National Forest. Why can't the race be today?

Some of my running friends advise me that at this point, less than a week before Old Dominion, if I had any sense I would be tapering off rather than risking injury pushing myself 16 miles on these trails, but the Big Dogs run this kind of mileage and more during the final week before they race, so why not me? Anyway, a few easy miles aren't going to wreck my entire summer. I haven't spent as much time running on the Uwharrie Trail this spring as I had originally planned. Spending all day in the woods is a good way to attune my mind to nature's rhythms.

June 1. The countdown to race day begins. I'm watching the five day forecast on the Weather Channel. The weather looks promising. No big storms in the forecast, temperatures in the 70's and 80's.

I have designed a Grand Slam Profile and mailed it out to the 40 ultrarunners who have finished the Big Four races. About 30 people have responded. The general advice I am getting from the profiles is to take the races one at a time.

Burgess Harmer of Reno, Nevada, advises, "Train hard, rest, and eat right. Don't let the GS control you - one race at a time at a pace you can stay healthy"

Barbara Ann Miller, of Modesto, California, writes, "Treat each 100 separately. Don't think of the GS as a whole. Think of it as a pie cut in four. Chip off each one and put it behind you. Each race is different, even if you've done them before. 100 miles is a long long way. Don't go out too fast or you'll be on the DNF list."

Lou Peyton of Little Rock, Arkansas, offers this advice, "It was a once in a lifetime challenge for me. I knew it was one special summer and all I had to do was reach the finish line. Time was not a problem... just keep on keeping on...Keep putting one foot in front of the other...Remember that all you want is to cross the finish line...the Grand Slam taught me to use my opportunities because sometimes you only get one chance to do a certain event. You'd better go for it when it is offered."

In the past, my problem at Old Dominion has been poor attitude — not taking the race seriously enough, not focusing on completing the race. I've been too concerned about the heat, and I have bad memories of my three DNFs in this event. It's important to turn all the negativism around this year and arrive in Woodstock with a positive outlook.

The challenge is to center my attention on the event before me and not get too wound up over one of the future races. To avoid the error of taking Old Dominion too lightly and looking ahead to Western States, I take out my OD course map, highlight the trails and the written instructions with a yellow marker, and pin the map on the wall in my office next to my desk.

Last minute doubts assail me. A runner the caliber of Dennis Herr of Harrisonburg, Virginia, who won Old Dominion in 1989 and has finished OD under 24 hours 7 times, attempted the Grand Slam twice and failed, DNFing Leadville in 1989 and Wasatch in 1990. Dennis has muscles coming out of his ears. His nickname is "The Animal." Who am I to think I can finish these four races when a man like Dennis couldn't?

Four members of my running club, the Fayetteville Area Runner's Association (FARA) — Mike Robertson, Carl Barshinger, Harvey Hall and myself — have entered Old Dominion this year but we won't run together. The other guys are all younger and faster than I am and will be in front of me. My three club mates are in the Army. Mike, the Old Dominion Run Secretary, and Harvey are physician's assistants in the 82nd Airborne Division. Carl is a Special Forces Sergeant at Fort Bragg. None of us has a crew, but Carl is trying to get his dad to come down from Pennsylvania to help him.

The excitement is building. Full throttle adrenalin is spreading through my body creating that special pre-race feeling of over-stimulation. Runners talk about their training peaking for a particular race, and that's how I feel. The fatigue and bad temper of the weeks of hard training are gone; they are replaced by nervousness, an inability to concentrate on anything that is not race-related, an excess of energy, an endorphin spillover, a desire to run the race NOW. It's time to eat that first piece of pie. LET'S GET IT ON!

Chapter 2

The Old Dominion 100 Mile Endurance Run.

Fortitudine Vicimus — "By Endurance We Conquer."

It is Springtime. Head for the Shenandoah!

Woodstock, Virginia, 4-5 June, 1994, George Washington National Forest. Weather forecast: temperatures in the mid-80's, humidity in the 70th percentile range, chance of rain.

Harvey, Carl, and I drive up to Virginia in Harv's van. Sharing the driving for the 6-1/2 hour trip, I don't feel tired and strung out like I do when driving long distances alone. Arriving in Woodstock, we check in at the Ramada Inn then head for the pre-race briefing across the highway at the Shenandoah County Fairgrounds.

Old Dominion is a down-home, low-key event. Nothing fancy. No hoopla. No hype. No sponsors' banners flying. The sole race momento we receive is a white, short-sleeved T-shirt with a red race logo on the front and the phrase, "It's hard to be humble when you've finished the Old Dominion," screened on the back.

The pre-race briefing is held in one of the metal buildings where, during the county fair, sheep are displayed and judged. The grandstand and dirt track where horses race are nearby. As 5 PM approaches and runners gather for the briefing, I feel like a dumb animal being led to slaughter.

My plan to weigh 165 lbs for the Grand Slam summer is a non-starter. Even after giving up chocolate ice cream for the past six weeks I weigh in at 177.

As he steps off the scale, Frank Probst, of Burke, Virginia, says, "Bob, I think the scale is 3 pounds heavy."

I respond, "Frank as far as I'm concerned, it's 12 pounds heavy."

At this point, all that matters is that on race day the medical check stations use the same scale as the one we weigh in on. This coordination is important because if medical staffers discover that a runner has lost 7% or more of his body weight during the race, he will be detained at the aid station until he eats and drinks enough to gain back some of his lost pounds. So, it's crucial that all the scales be accurate since no one wants to be held up. If the runner is badly dehydrated and in really rough shape, he will be pulled from the race.

Sixty-two athletes, including 5 women, from 21 states and Canada have gathered in Woodstock for the 16th Annual Old Dominion 100. Many of them are feeling vulnerable, anxious, uneasily aware of their own mortality.

After we collect our race numbers (mine is 37), Pat Botts welcomes everyone to the Shenandoah Valley. The briefing is short and to the point — mainly a description of the course and the rules of the race. A runner who goes off course must return to his point of departure via the same route he took when he got lost; anyone who accepts a ride will be disqualified; everyone has to weigh in and cooperate with the volunteers at the medical check points; no littering; and no smoking on the course by anyone, crew or runner.

Deaf runner, King Jordan, sits on the floor reading the briefer's lips while his wife, Marsha, perches in front of him signing rapidly. I'm not paying much attention until an announcement is made that wakes me up. Energy drinks and Coke will be available at the aid stations, but no water. I feel stunned, like someone has whacked me on the back of the head with a shovel. This is breathtaking. What the hell is going on? No water at an event renowned for its hot and humid conditions? It turns out to be a false alarm, but my anxiety level shoots up like a Saturn IV rocket at Cape Canaveral.

Following the briefing, I join friends for a vegetarian lasagna supper. The pre-race sharing of bread and pasta is one of the many cult practices of 100 mile trail runners. After supper I celebrate another of our rituals. Alone in my motel room, I shower, towel myself dry, then lather up a two inch circle around each of my nipples. A Gillette razor is reserved specially for this ceremony.

Muttering a pious incantation, I shave all the hair around each nipple, tricky work because of the tenderness of the area. Finally, I place a band-aid across each nipple making sure that the nipple itself is in the precise center of the band-aid.

I also place band-aids on sensitive areas along the edge of my latissimus dorsi muscle, just under each arm pit. The bandaging is designed to prevent chaffing. I then consume one chocolate Powerbar, washing it down with a potent mixture of high carbohydrate energy drink and Mountain Dew. Only when the last morsel of Powerbar is choked down am I satisfied that the ritual has been successful and that I will have a dynamic run the next day.

Sitting quietly in my motel room, I formulate my race action plan. Based on previous year's times, I figure that if I reach Hecht's Farm between 8 and 9 AM, 4 Corners at around 1 PM, Elizabeth Furnace in the vicinity of 8 PM, and the bottom of Veach Gap circa 1 AM, in other words, 9—1—8—1, I can finish OD in under 24 hours. I'm not going to push myself to achieve that goal, but I will keep those times in mind, just in case I'm close and have a good energy level during the last 20 miles. My main objective is to finish under the 28 hour time limit and not trash myself.

Rising at 3 AM following an unusually sound five hours of sleep, I manage to ingest a banana, some yogurt and another Powerbar, flushed down with Coke in preparation for the challenge ahead. Another esoteric rite now takes place — the lotioning of the feet. For this procedure I have combined five ingredients — vaseline petroleum jelly, vitamin A and D cream, Desitin diaper rash ointment, vitamin E cream, and aloe vera cream. Reverentially, I ooze the stuff between the toes and around the heels. The idea is that these lotional charms will have the desired magical effect and blisters will not arise from my feet during the race.

Normally, I wear well broken-in Nike Air Pegasus shoes, but in honor of the Grand Slam I have invested $85.00 in a pair of Adidas Trail Response shoes, size 12, which I pull on over thin polypropolene socks. The shoelaces are doubled knotted so they don't come loose during the race, and they are pulled loosely rather than tightly leaving my feet room to swell in the shoes.

Having slept in my Pategonia nylon running shorts and Uwharrie Adventure Run t-shirt, all I need do is tie a red bandana around my neck, put on my white visored cap, strap on my fanny pack with its two 20-ounce plastic bottles filled with the energy drink/ Mountain Dew mixture, and I am ready to race.

The pack is a Western States 100 model with two zippered side pockets (useful for carrying hard candies) and a butt pocket large enough for two Powerbars, a Garrity Life Lite, and some toilet paper in a plastic sandwich baggie. The Garrity Life Lite is a small flashlight which sells for less than $2.00 at Wal Mart. Half the size of my hand, it fits nicely into the butt pocket; it is light weight, throws a decent beam, and lasts longer than other lights I have tried.

Unable to recruit a crew or pacer for this race, I am relying on six drop bags containing 8-oz cans of chocolate flavored Ensure Plus (a liquid food supplement); 16-oz bottles of Mountain Dew (loaded with sugar and caffeine); extra 20-oz. bottles of carbohydrate-rich energy drink; additional Garrity Life Lites; my goretex jacket; plus changes of shirts and caps. One Ensure Plus can contains 355 calories and is the equivalent of a small meal. I depend on it, the Mountain Dew, and the energy drink for most of my fuel during the race.

For this race, pacers (also referred to as companion runners) are only allowed for the section from Elizabeth Furnace to the bottom of Veach Gap, roughly between the 75 and 88 mile points. Having trudged over these trails numerous times in the past, I know the course so I won't need any help.

Not having a crew doesn't bother me. Crews can help or hinder the runner. Peter Gagarin of *UltraRunning* magazine once suggested that anyone making it through a 100-miler successfully without a handler should have an hour taken off his time. Peter feels that having a crew gives the runner a physical edge because he will eat and drink more, a plus in efficiency because the crew will take care of his needs quickly; additionally, there is the psychological bonus of just seeing a friendly face.

I'll buy the friendly face argument, but crews and pacers complicate these events, and I like to keep my race as simple as I can. The possibility exists that handlers will get lost moving from aid station to aid station and not be there for the runner at a crucial time. This absence can have a devastating effect on the runner who has been looking forward to being helped by his crew. Crews also get tired and grouchy just like runners. Negative crew attitudes can bring a runner down, leading to his withdrawal from the race. And the presence of a friendly crew and convenient vehicle to carry the runner back to the motel with its beckoning bed and shower can be a powerful stimulant to dropping out if the athlete feels like quitting.

Carl's dad has arrived so he will crew for Carl and Harvey. They will be several hours ahead of me, so it won't be convenient for him to help me. I know a lot of the crews for other runners and am friends with many of the volunteers at the aid stations, so I feel confident that if I crash, someone will be there to take care of me.

Four AM sharp. A short prayer followed by a shotgun blast, the music from Chariots of Fire, Timex watches are punched, and we're off; two laps around the Shenandoah County Fairgrounds dirt race track then out onto the streets of Woodstock. Woodstock is famous as the place where, one Sunday morning in 1775, Lutheran Pastor John Peter Muhlenberg preached a final sermon then removed his clerical robe to reveal the uniform of a colonel in the Revolutionary Army. With the words, "There is a time to pray and a time to fight," he mobilized 300 recruits from his congregation to march against the British colonial troops.

The atmosphere at the start of the race is similar to the wartime hysteria which swept the small town 219 years ago. The runners are jacked up sky high on caffeine and adrenalin. Yelling, yodeling, and yahooing reverberate through the quiet streets of Woodstock. Keeping myself under control, I gravitate to the back of the pack. The police vehicle leading the front runners disappears, its lights flashing.

This misty morning finds me trotting along with Jerry Tanner who lives in Fort Valley. Our flashlight beams and soft footfalls bounce off the pavement in matching time. A few miles into the race David Powell, of Alexandria, Virginia, comes hurtling back toward us wildeyed and shouting.

"The course isn't marked. We're going the wrong way."

The first 28.1 miles of the Old Dominion course are on roads and, as far as Jerry and I can determine, we haven't strayed off them yet. David vanishes into the night before either of us can stop and reassure him that everything is fine. Having finished Old Dominion under 24 hours eight times previously, David knows the course as well as anyone. I have no idea what spooked him.

Fireflies blanket the quiet fields outside of town, each one marking its small piece of territory. Blessed by the maiden blush of morning, we cross the North Fork of the Shenandoah River on Burnshire Bridge. At the 7-mile point, we commence the first major climb of the day, to the top of Powell Mountain up a switchback gravel road.

In their exhuberance, many of the competitors run up the mountain, Jerry among them. These are people who want to put some "easy" miles in the bank before being slowed by the heat of the day. I am content to powerwalk this stretch of road to conserve energy for the long haul.

On the other side of Powell Mountain, Fort Valley welcomes us with the sweet perfume of honeysuckle and freshly mown hay. Shaped like a long banana, Fort Valley extends roughly 60 miles from southwest to northeast and measures about 4 miles at its widest point. Bordered on the southeast by Massanutten Mountain and on the northwest by a series of wooded ridges — Short Mountain, Powell Mountain, and Three Top Mountain — the valley is entered through gaps — Shawl Gap, Veach Gap, Milford Gap, Hebron Gap from the Massanutten side and Mudhole Gap, Mine Gap, Woodstock Gap, and Edinburg Gap through Powell Mountain and Three Top Mountain.

The South Fork of the Shenandoah River lies to the east of Massanutten Mountain, and the North Fork of the Shenandoah curls west of Powell Mountain. Passage Creek flows in a northeasterly direction down the center of Fort Valley before emptying into the Shenandoah on its northward journey to the Potomac.

The same families have occupied Fort Valley farms for generations. Newcomers tend to build their houses on the southeast-facing mountain slopes. The Old Dominion 100 course crosses Fort Valley four times and, in between, follows ridge lines north or south.

Hastening along country lanes, runners salute dairy cattle, their udders swollen in the coolness of morning. As we pass through Mine Gap, the course turns east then south; it intersects State Road 678, the main north-south thoroughfare; then the course meanders across the peaceful valley toward Massanutten Mountain.

25

As always, Rick Hogan lays back in the early stages of the race, catching up to me at the 25 mile point. It happens this way every year. Like all successful ultramarathoners, Rick is a strong walker.

"Morning, Rick." I am forced to run to keep up with his powerwalk.

"Hello, Bob." Unusually taciturn, Rick is all business today. Encountering a series of short steep hills, I give up trying to maintain his pace. Rick teaches philosophy at the University of Massachusetts. His record of eleven straight finishes at Old Dominion, all under 24 hours, is a marvel of courage, consistency, and devotion to Friedrich Nietzsche's dictum, "What does not kill me makes me stronger."

Rick arrives at Hecht's Farm, the 28 mile aid station, shortly after 9:00 AM. I am right behind him, on the cusp of my 24-hour finish plan. We don't linger at Hecht's, but quickly enter the forest for the second major climb of the day to the top of Massanutten Mountain. The foot trail switchbacks sharply up the flank of the mountain through stands of mountain laurel and yellow pine. Reaching the crest of the ridge, we hurry along a narrow, rocky, orange-blazed path catching glimpses of the morning sun glinting off the Shenandoah River far below.

At the front of the race a trio of runners leads the way. Liberty University professor, David Horton, 44, of Lynchburg, Virginia, — Mountain Masochist 50 mile race director, Applachian Trail record holder, and three time winner of this event — is shadowed by two newcomers, 22-year-old Mike Morton, a Navy diver stationed in Norfolk, Virginia, and Courtney Campbell, 29, who coaches high school track in Berryville, a small town near Winchester, Virginia.

Between them, Morton and Campbell have a grand total of three ultras under their belts, none longer than 50 miles. Their plan is to play the waiting game, dog Horton's footsteps, work together, and stay with the veteran as long as they can. Horton is iron- willed and runs to win, but has been troubled in the past by a delicate stomach. Chances are excellent that the heat and humidity, rocky trails, and vicious climbs and descents will knock out the rookies and David will prevail once again.

A scurry of trail runners follows the leaders. This group includes the top women, Edith Bogenhuber, 49 of San Mateo, California, and Pat Botts, 54, who has been suffering from a *plantar fasciitis* injury (pain on the bottom of the foot directly in front of the heel). The discomfort is caused by inflammation at the point where the plantar fascia ligament joins the heel. Usually, this is a nagging injury which only heals after several months of complete rest: in other words, no running.

Others in the chase include Andy Peterson, 37 from nearby Luray, Virginia, who runs in black socks; all three of my FARA ultrarunning teammates - Carl, Mike and Harvey; Steve Schiller, 37, of New Britain, Connecticut, the 1993 OD champ, who is a 1994 Grand Slam candidate; another '94 Grand Slam hopeful, Larry Ochsendorf, 49, of Apple Valley, Minnesota; Gary Berkner, 42, of Alexandria, Virginia; and Mike Fiorito, 27, of Apex, North Carolina.

Skirting Kennedy's Peak, competitors dash into the first medical check at Camp Roosevelt (35.1 miles), site of the first New Deal Civilian Conservation Corporation camp built in the 1930's. I weigh in at 178, one pound over my pre-race figure. Just right. I am hydrating properly. Snatching a handful of pretzels and a cup of Coke, I charge out of the aid station.

This race is all about fighting off the heat. A bandana protects my neck. The white, long-sleeved shirt and white hat I wear reflect the sun. I carry three plastic water bottles and slug fluids at every opportunity. In addition, I carry a small towel which I soak in creeks along the course and apply to my groin, armpits, and neck where major blood vessels come close to the surface. The wet towel cools the blood vessels, thus keeping my body temperature down, lessening the possibility of heatstroke. I drape the wet towel across my shoulders afterwards.

My precautions work; I'm running comfortably. It helps that the humidity level is moderate and that the temperature is "only" 85, not as hot as it can be at Old Dominion on race day.

After Camp Roosevelt, runners encounter the difficult Duncan Hollow Trail, "the slowest seven miles in east coast trail running." In Duncan Hollow I catch up with Eugene Ellenbogen, a South African by way of Toronto, Canada. Old Dominion is Eugene's maiden 100 miler, and he is not happy. He has lost 6 pounds and dehydration is causing cramps in the quadricep muscle of his left leg. Fascinated, I study the involuntary muscle twitching knowing that if Eugene does not rehydrate, his race will soon be over.

As we stumble along the rocky corridor insects torment us. Thorn bushes clutch at our feet and legs. Springs bubbling off the slopes of Catback Mountain muck up the trail increasing Eugene's irritation. Stopping to wet my towel, I suggest that he sit in the water to cool his legs. He snaps at me that he doesnt want to get his "bloody expensive shoes soaked." I try an ultrarunner's joke to cheer Eugene up.

"What's the German word for constipation?"

"How should I know?" Eugene is in no mood to play games.

"Fahrfrumpupen."

Laughing, I sprint ahead. Grimacing in discomfort, Eugene increases his speed to match mine.

"*Jy praat twak*, Bob."

"What's that mean?"

"'You're talking nonsense,' man. In Afrikaans. Do you know what the Chinese word for constipation is?"

"No, I don't, Eugene."

"Hung chow."

Walnut, hickory, and oak trees flourish in Duncan Hollow. After passing Duncan Knob, at over 2800 feet the highest point on the Old Dominion course, we turn sharply to the north on Scothorne Gap Trail. Finally, escaping from the heathen pathway, Eugene and I wade through Passage Creek, pause a moment to wash off our arms and legs, then turn right onto Chrisman Hollow Road. This is the 42.8 mile point, but it feels like 50. The gravel road presents an opportunity to make up time lost in Duncan Hollow, but with no protection from the blazing mid-day sun, we struggle to quicken the pace.

Passing vehicles kick up dust in the heat. Eugene and I join Cindy Grunt of Welches, Oregon, who is also beginning her Grand Slam quest. Cindy tried the Slam last year, but didn't finish Leadville. She is only 5'2", which means she takes twice as many steps as I do to cover the same distance. I call her "sewing machine legs" for her rapid leg turnover.

Cindy, Eugene, and I stay together through the 4 Points aid station at the 47 mile mark. 4 Points is a shady crossroads, a good place for crews to wait for their runners. In 1993 I wasted a lot of time visiting with the aid station personnel; then a half mile down

28

Cindy Grunt, class of 1994, looking confident before Wasatch Front.

by Robert Boeder

the road I took a wrong turn, went off the course, and DNFed. The DNF was my own fault for not carrying a map.

Getting lost in 1993 still rankles, but I learned from my mistake. Goofing off at the wrong time cost me my race, so I have adopted a more serious approach dedicated to finishing this and all future Old Dominions. The only acceptable reasons for quitting in 1994 are total exhaustion or career threatening injury.

Anger is an excellent motivator. Today I'm still mad at myself and don't repeat the mistakes of 1993. Refusing to sit down, I take care of business, quickly downing my energy drinks and pouring cold water over my head and shoulders to cool off before departing the aid station.

The correct race route propels us uphill on paved Highway 730 beside Mountain Run stream. Cindy runs the ascents better than I, and she moves ahead. Eugene's legs are cramping continually now, and he falls behind. Reaching the half way point in 10 hours and 30 minutes, I am pleased with myself for maintaining my 24-hour finishing pace.

As I turn north on Little Fort Road in the hottest part of the day, the sun pounds like a sledgehammer on my neck and shoulders. Little Fort Road ascends to Taskers Gap then plunges downhill toward Edinburg Gap. Along the way, I catch up with 1992 Grand Slammer, Lee "El Burro" Schmidt, of Palo Alto, California.

You can't miss Lee. With his shoulder-length white hair and multiple earings, he looks like the mad scientist in the *Back To The Future* movies. Lee is never without his trademark Australian bush hat, with the brim rolled up on the sides, and his sleeveless shirt that looks like it has survived a million spin cycles. Lee was given his nickname by a friend who said he resembled a grizzled, old hermit prospector living in the mountains — alone, anti-social, and stubborn — with only his burro for company. At this point in the race a hip problem has hobbled him. I hustle past, knowing that Lee's remarkable recuperative powers will soon kick in and he will eventually run me down.

Until Edinburg Gap, the 56 mile point, my race has been going very well. I have been running easily, walking the uphills, staying hydrated. But it doesn't matter how experienced I am or how many 100-mile races I enter, I always commit at least one major tactical error.

My 1994 Old Dominion boner is not leaving a drop bag at Edinburgh Gap, which means I miss my cans of Ensure Plus and Mountain Dew at this crucial aid station. The aid stations at Old Dominion are well supplied, but without these vital calorie supplements I experience an energy swoon on the next 8 mile section, a very rough gravel road designed for All Terrain Vehicle races.

The ATV track — nasty, rugged and steep — inches up the corrugated side of Opechee Peak. Sure enough, "El Burro" hurtles by as my careful plan for a 24 hour finish evaporates. I begin to alternate walking with running then slip into the Boeder Shuffle which eventually becomes a butt dragging slog.

I sink into a deep funk, the antithesis of "runner's high," the endorphin rush experienced in shorter races. This evil twin is "runner's low," the depressed state we fall into at some point in every 100-miler when all the energy has been sucked out of us. Right now I could care less about a 24-hour finish. I feel lousy.

While mumbling and grumbling, feeling sorry for myself, David Powell swoops past.

"David, where did you come from?" I yell, feeling uncharitable.

"I want to finish in under 24 hours," he replies, disappearing down the road.

I haven't the slightest clue about what or who convinced David to re-enter the race after his morning panic attack. Apparently he wants to keep his finishing record intact. I wish him well without much enthusiasm. David is not like other mortals. He often runs negative splits in these races; that is, he covers the second half of the course faster than the first half. He doesn't always carry water bottles between aid stations. David doesn't eat much during competition either, and he drinks mainly Pepsi Cola to keep his energy level up.

Most runners pray for cloud cover along this stretch of gravel road. Ferocious late afternoon hail and lightning thunderstorms are common. Today, nothing happens. A few flies divebomb me as I stagger past Peter's Mill Pond on my unmerry way to Little Fort Campground.

Little Fort Campground aid station (63.6 miles) is always a welcome sight — so much so that it is a favorite place to quit. In 1992, my friend, Herman Forbes, of Burlington, North Carolina,

31

dropped out at Little Fort after vomiting the cheese pizza he was eating. At Little Fort in 1993, another North Carolina runner of my acquaintance was informed by his girl friend, crewing for him, that their romance was at an end. He threw in the towel. Life goes on, even during a 100-mile trail race.

Somehow I resist the urge to quit. Delving into my drop bag, I struggle to tear off the pop top of a can of Ensure Plus. The liquid goes down easily. Gulping my energy drink and Mountain Dew, I wolf down some chocolate chip cookies; then, I'm off.

Forest Service Road 273 takes me north through Little Fort Valley between Three Top Mountain and Green Mountain and finally delivers me at Mudhole Gap (68.7 miles) aid station early in the evening. This aid station is manned by a bunch of weight lifters from the Woodstock version of Gold's Gym. I like these guys. Their energy is infectious and I feel better after joking around with them. The calories from my liquid meal at Little Fort are beginning to kick in as well, and I feel strong again, ready to do some running.

The next section is one of the prettiest parts of the Old Dominion course. Too bad it's after dark and I can't enjoy the scenery. Following a gradual descent on an old logging road, I lose track of the number of times I splash through Little Passage Creek. Finally, after careening downhill through the woods on Bear Wallow Spur Trail and Big Blue Trail, I cross Highway 678, the Valley Road; I traverse a bridge over Passage Creek and pull into Elizabeth Furnace Picnic Area. This is the site of one of three pre-Civil War iron smelters in Fort Valley - the others are Caroline Furnace and Boyer Furnace.

Elizabeth Furnace is the 74.6 mile aid station, the second and final medical check and the only point on the course with a cutoff time — 12 midnight. It's just after 9 PM, an hour past my target time to meet my 24-hour goal. Any chance of breaking 24 hours has evaporated. I'm actually relieved since now I don't have to exhaust myself in a mad dash to finish before 4:00 AM. Better to conserve my energy for Western States.

With 11 hours remaining to travel the 25 miles to the finish, I can make it easily, even worming along at less than 3 miles per hour. At Elizabeth Furnace, I take a few extra minutes to put on a clean, long sleeved capilene shirt and my goretex jacket in preparation for the cool night ahead. After making sure that my flashlight works and that I have an extra one in my fanny pack, I drink several cups of Coke and eat a banana to get stoked for the punishment that lies ahead.

Many Old Dominion competitors pick Elizabeth Furnace as the place to say "to hell with it" and drop out, aware that the infamous ascent of Sherman Gap awaits them. Nobody seems to know exactly who Sherman was, but Pat Botts swears he was the first runner to try to run this section of trail. Local lore places his grave ten feet from the top of the gap.

The 12 miles from Elizabeth Furnace to the bottom of Veach Gap (86.6 miles) is the only part of the race where pacers are permitted. This is a safety precaution because most runners traverse this stretch after dark. Violent storms are common on June nights in this part of Virginia, and the trail is rocky and rough, definitely not a place to be lost or hurt. Chemlights hang from tree branches every so often to light the way, giving runners confidence that they are on the right path.

The only time I ever traversed Sherman Gap in daylight was in 1989 when I paced Vicki Johnson to her Old Dominion women's record of 20:47. A great trail runner, Vicki combined toughness with a warm and gregarious personality. I have fond memories of that night five years ago.

Today, ten hours earlier, Mike Morton and Courtney Campbell caught up with and passed a flagging David Horton climbing to the top of Sherman Gap. At the same time as I depart Elizabeth Furnace and steal into the woods along Passage Creek, Morton and Campbell are crossing the finish line the race winners in 17:40:29. They have earned their rest while I continue to struggle through the night.

Crossing Sherman Gap takes me three hours. This section of the course has been named Botts Trail in honor of Pat's late husband. A stone monument dedicated to Wayne Botts has been built at the bottom of the climb. The ascent interminably meanders through an exhausting cluster of false summits until finally straightening out and coming close to vertical towards the top.

A runner passes me on his way back down to Elizabeth Furnace. He has not reached the crest of the Gap.

"What's wrong?" I ask.

"The climb is too much for me. I'm going back to the aid station to drop out."

He's not limping; he doesn't appear to be hurt; he doesn't even look tired. He has given up mentally. I don't encourage him to continue. All of my energy is focused on my own effort.

Summitting, I am elated. Tears come to my eyes as a wave of emotion engulfs me. There is no one to hug so I hug myself.

"Way to go, Bob, I'm proud of you."

Blowing my dripping nose with my fingers, I hurry along the ridge top following the chemlights beckoning me toward the long steep downhill. This is a tricky and treacherous stretch where fatigue can cause a runner to stumble and sprawl headfirst into the rocks.

I'm worn out and losing control of my emotions The joy felt a few minutes before at the top of Sherman Gap turns to fear. The specter of failure haunts me in the darkness. In this situation, tripping and falling on these steep slopes at night can be a deathblow to one's hopes of finishing. Becoming injured while exhausted is like a pin popping a balloon. All desire to finish vanishes in a split second.

It's midnight when I finally reach Fish Hatchery Road, the gravel by-way that parallels the North Fork of the Shenandoah. Beneath a thin crescent moon, the clear call of a whippoorwill sounds like a ghostly beacon in the night. A nest of chemlights on my right announces the next aid station, Veach East, where the volunteers act giddy, sleep deprived.

The hike to the top of Veach Gap follows a wagon road built by General Daniel Morgan during the Revolutionary War as an escape route in case Washington's army was forced to retreat. Morgan's road has been disfigured by trenches dug every 15-20 feet by the National Forest staff as anti-erosion measures to carry run-off down the mountainside. The ditches are like outsized furrows, virtual tank traps, gauged in the side of the mountain. At the top of Veach Gap, ribbons indicate a right turn.

My idea of hell is to spend eternity careening blindfolded, barefoot, and naked in a headlong charge down the west side of Veach Gap at midnight during a torrential downpour. Tonight it isn't raining, but it's cold and I'm shivering despite wearing a long sleeved shirt, knit cap, and jacket. I descend like Dante through a brutal boulder fall, a bone dry creek bed, and more dangerous anti-erosion channels.

On my way to the bottom of the gap I nearly trip over a pair of legs. It's the prostrate form of Jerry Tanner. Suffering from dehydration and clad only in a t-shirt and shorts, he has collapsed in the middle of the trail. I am concerned that Jerry's core body temperature will drop and that he will become hypothermic in the cold damp air, but I can't help him. He needs a blanket and some hot soup. Arriving at the Veach West aid station 15 minutes later, I inform the volunteers, who quickly move up the mountain to assist Jerry.

Four AM. Four hours to travel 12.2 miles. After Veach, the course returns to country lanes, mostly gravel, some paved, well marked and easy to follow with chemlights pointing the way. In previous years, local yokels with names like "Indian Bob" amused themselves by moving ribbons and chemlights so as to direct runners into cul de sacs and off the edges of cliffs. No one was hurt, but a few competitors DNFed because they got lost. This year, "Indian Bob" has been warned to stay home. Law enforcement officers patrol the course. All is quiet.

Plodding toward Woodstock, exhausted and alone in the blackness, a primal sadness envelops me. Tears fill my eyes. Sobs well up as if something deep inside is coming apart, but as quickly as the emotion arises, it passes. Crying is cathartic. I feel better. No one witnessed my little breakdown. Eating a chocolate chip cookie and drinking a cup of Coke at the next aid station invite sugar into my bloodstream.

Hobbling to the top of Woodstock Gap I catch another runner, Stuart White, from Great Falls, Montana. Stuart is falling asleep on his feet. Drowsy myself, I chatter to keep both of us awake. Stuart's brother is waiting for him at the Mountain Top aid station near the summit of the Gap. Eight miles remain. I push on by myself, sore-legged, tender footed, fighting the temptation to lie down and take a nap.

Home stretch now, coming down the west side of Powell Mountain on the switchback gravel road. The sky brightens at Burnshire Bridge, the same place it did 24 hours ago when I was heading in the opposite direction. During these final miles as I descend the mountain and stop for a Coke at the 97.2 mile Water

Street aid station and enter Woodstock, I keep looking back to see if anyone is gaining on me. Each time the road is empty. Suddenly, on Ox Road, with less than a mile remaining, a runner looking as fresh as a dewdrop lopes past me.

This fellow definitely does not appear to have just run 99 miles. He calls out a hearty good morning. I can't work up the effort to be sarcastic at 6 AM, so I just let him run in while I walk, tortoise-like, into the Fairgrounds, circle the track, and cross the finish line.

No cheering throngs greet me, no brass bands. In fact, the only person present is Henry Muhlbauer, the official timer, who videotapes me as I pass under the finish banner. After we shake hands, Henry tells me I am the 34th finisher. My time is 26:31:07, a personal best for Old Dominion.

The lack of celebration at the completion of the race is anticlimactic, but finishing is its own reward, and I'm fiercely proud of myself for what I have accomplished. The first hurdle in the Grand Slam has been cleared. Bring on Western States.

I think of the OD motto,"It's hard to be humble when you've finished The Old Dominion," but all I feel is tired as I drag myself back to the Ramada Inn at 7 AM on the already warm Sunday morning.

Back in the motel room, I shower then rub down my legs with Sports Creme. My bodily fluids have pooled in my extremities, so I place ice packs on my swollen hands, feet, and ankles. Examining my feet, I find blisters on both second toes and on my heels. The shoes I wore should have been a half size larger.

The race ends at 8 AM and the awards ceremony takes place a half hour later in the Grandstand. Forty runners have endured the entire 100 miles. Finishers in under 24 hours receive belt buckles; those completing the event in less than 28 hours get plaques.

At 22 and 29 years of age, Mike Morton and Courtney Campbell shatter the common notion that young men do not have the mental toughness to excel at ultrarunning. They represent a new generation of East Coast trail runners, having dethroned David Horton, one of the high priests of the ultra world. No small achievement.

Edith Bogenhuber comes in tenth overall in 21:45:14 to win the women's race. Pat Botts takes second in 23:40:38. Pat's daughter,

Wynne, and son-in-law, Ray Waldron, direct the Old Dominion 100.

Rick Hogan wins his twelfth straight buckle in 23:51:58. David Powell falls excrutiatingly short of buckling but still runs well in 24:03:22.

At Old Dominion, runners are not pulled from the race at aid stations if they have no chance of finishing in under 28 hours. While the awards are being handed out, Steve Bozeman of Lynchburg, Virginia, crosses the finish line. He is not an official finisher, but because a crowd has gathered for the awards he receives what Mike Robertson calls "the biggest finishing ovation in the history of the OD 100."

The FARA ultrarunning team has done well. Harvey finished third overall in 19:31:57, Mike came in sixth in 20:58:44, and Carl Barshinger's time of 23:41 wins him a buckle.

Among my fellow Grand Slam candidates, Dixie Madsen, of San Diego, California, completes the race in 27:48:11, just barely inside the 28 hour limit. Cindi Grunt has a strong second half and buckles in 23:45:36. Lee Schmidt is agonizingly close to buckling but misses by less than a minute in 24:00:57. Larry Ochsendorf is the fastest Grand Slam candidate in 20:58:46.

After the awards ceremony, I introduce myself to Burgess Harmer. I am in awe of Burgess, going for his fourth Eagle in Flight statue, the trophy awarded to successful Grand Slammers. Burgess is 52, 6'2", 180 lbs, and ran a fast time (22:38:01) at OD. The other Old Dominion runners who have announced their intentions to complete the Grand Slam in 1994 are Maurice Beaulieu, from Vancouver, British Columbia (23:48:33), Steve Schiller (21:29:33), and Luther Thompson of Woodbury, Minnesota, (22:54:39). Nine of us. How many will be left by Wasatch?

Grand Slam Gorilla, Burgess Harmer, relaxing before Wasatch.

by Robert Boeder

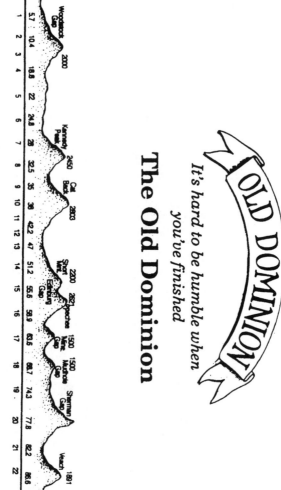

OLD DOMINION

*It's hard to be humble when
you've finished*

The Old Dominion

39

Chapter 3

The Western States 100 Mile Endurance Run.

100 Miles. One Day.

Squaw Valley, California, June 25-26, 1994, Granite Chief Wilderness Area, Tahoe and El Dorado National Forests. Weather: sunny, daytime temperatures in the mid-80's.

Inspirational quote from Theodore Roosevelt in the Western States Participant's Guide:

"It is not the critic who counts, not the man who points out how the strong man stumbled, or where the doer of deeds could have done them better. The credit belongs to the man who is actually in the arena; whose face is marred by dust and sweat and blood; who strives valiantly, who errs and comes short again and again; who knows the great enthusiasms, the great devotions, and spends himself in a worthy cause; who, at the best, knows in the end the triumph of high achievement; and who, at the worst, at least fails while daring greatly, so that his place shall never be with those cold and timid souls who know neither victory nor defeat."

Usually, I "live the race" for a week or ten days afterward. The euphoria takes that long to wear off, but this year I only devote a few days to self-congratulation before putting Old Dominion behind and switching my focus to Western States. I'm worried about my feet, so I telephone Grand Slammer, Marshall Ulrich, of Fort Morgan, Colorado, for advice. With his multi-day journey run and 100 mile race experience, he should know about proper foot care.

Marshall is concise: "Bob, I have three suggestions for you: train in the same shoes you wear during the race; wear two pairs of socks, either both made of polypropolene fabric or one polypro and a thicker sock like a Thorlo; and rub an entire tube of lanolin into your feet before the race followed by a layer of vasoline."

I'm embarrassed. I have been training in Nikes and racing in Adidas. That must be the problem. I've never tried wearing two pairs of socks.

Since Old Dominion, I have cut back on training to some extent, not running as many miles and not working out on my machines every night. On June 14 and 16 I participate in the Fort Bragg Track Meet 2 and 3 mile runs. My times are 40 seconds faster than last year when I was the Fort Bragg 3 mile masters division champion, but this year there is more competition, and I fail to place in my age group. On Saturday I venture into the Uwharrie Forest for a 16 mile out-and-back trail run. My experiment with a new energy drink that is supposed to contain 700 calories in 22 ounces of fluid doesn't work, and I die on the return 8 mile leg.

Over the weekend of June 18-19, I start to get pumped for Western States. It's hot (in the 90's) and humid in Fayetteville during the two weeks after OD. Watching the weather reports for Sacramento and the Sierras, I note that practically every low temperature in the nation for the last week is recorded in Truckee, California, just down the road from Squaw Valley where Western States starts. These lows are in the teens and low 20's, so it looks like it will be cold, at least at the beginning of the race. Temperatures for Sacramento range from the high 40's to the mid-80's. On Monday, June 20, the weather outlook for race weekend in the California mountains calls for 70 and 80 degree temperatures.

Western States race co-director, Norm Klein, is fanatical about statistics, so WS runners receive complete split times following the race. Two large printouts are mailed — one records the real time arrival and departure from nine aid stations and the place of each runner at the aid station, plus the real finish time and total time. The other provides a record of times between the ten main check points plus the place of each runner in comparison with other runners in that particular section.

I enjoy pouring over these numbers to compare myself with other runners. For example, in 1993, I finished 202nd overall in 29:44:35 at Western, but I ran the last 6.6 miles from Highway 49 to the finish almost an hour faster than Fred Shufflebarger, who finished 19th overall in 21:59:53. So what? It means that I had to hustle to finish in under 30 hours and Fred didn't. This year my goal is to improve on last year's time. I want to go under 28 hours.

Wednesday, June 22. After placing third at Old Dominion, Harvey Hall volunteers to serve as my combination crew and pacer at Western States. I am relieved. I suspect that part of my emotional upheaval in the latter stages of OD was the result of not having a crew, of feeling abandoned.

We rise early to drive to Raleigh-Durham International Airport to catch the short hop to Charlotte where we change planes for the five hour flight to the west coast. The last portion of our journey takes us over Mono Lake, the Sierra Nevada Mountains, and Yosemite National Park before we touch down at San Francisco International Airport. The views are fabulous from 35,000 feet. This spectacularly beautiful but harsh terrain is similar to that covered by the Western States Trail.

I'm anxious to reach Tahoe City, California, where we will be staying before the race, so we don't waste time sightseeing in San Francisco. Harvey maneuvers our rental car across the Bay Bridge on Interstate 80, through Oakland, Sacramento, Auburn (where the race finishes), and Truckee. During the five hour drive I begin my usual pre-100-mile race process of blocking out extraneous matters, withdrawing mentally to husband my strength for the upcoming ordeal.

Our destination is the Family Tree Motel in Tahoe City. The motel is easy to find because it is right across from a huge pine tree growing in the middle of Highway 28, the only street in town. Although the bathroom ventilation at the Family Tree leaves something to be desired, the price is right and an equally moderately priced restaurant is nearby.

Thursday, June 23. After carbo loading on breakfast pancakes at the Family Tree Restaurant, Harv and I head for Squaw Valley. 1960 Olympic rings welcome us as we enter the famed resort where empty chalets await winter snows. Squaw Mountain looms at the head of the valley. Snowmelt from surrounding peaks feeds a sparkling stream. For centuries, Washoe Indian families migrated from Lake Tahoe to set up their summer hunting camps in this verdant valley.

Today we are here for one of the pre-race activities, the trek to the flag raising at the top of Emigrant Pass. We have three choices of transportation to the summit: running, walking, or riding a tram. The tram ride costs $10. Although it's close to race day and I want to conserve energy, I feel I will get stale without some exercise so we decide to walk.

Our route follows the race course beginning next to the tram building on the valley floor at 6,200 feet above sea level and ascending to top of Emigrant Pass at 8,700 feet, a climb of 2,500 vertical feet in a distance of 4 1/2 miles. This is my third time at Western States; Harv was born and raised in Southern California, but this is his first visit to Squaw Valley.

At noon, a small crowd gathers at the top of the pass near Watson's Monument, a rock obelisk commemorating Robert Montgomery Watson, "Trailfinder of the Sierra," the man who, in 1931, rediscovered and marked the Emigrant Road section of the Western States Trail used by 19th century miners traveling from the silver lodes of Nevada to the gold diggings of Northern California. A 40-mile-per-hour wind blasts the summit, so most of us huddle on the leeward side of the pass while Western States Endurance Run Foundation board members Tony Rossmann and Mo Livermore present their inspirational remarks.

The purpose of our gathering is to remember friends of Western States who have died during the past year. My Dad was never part of Western States and he never saw me run 100 miles, but he passed away on September 26, 1993, so I take the opportunity in this wild place to tell him that I miss him and that I know he is proud of me.

Most of what Tony and Mo have to say is about Barbara Schoener, a trailrunner who this past April was attacked and killed by a cougar while on a training run on the Auburn Lake Trails section of the Western States course. Apparently, the young cat jumped Barbara from behind when she was running alone and knocked her down a slope then attacked her again. A week later California State Fish and Game officials trapped and killed the animal. A baby cougar was discovered nearby.

Ironically, the cougar is the symbol of Western States. A likeness of the animal graces the race logo found on everything connected to the event, from T-shirts to belt buckles to plastic water bottles.

Also known as mountain lions, panthers and pumas, cougars rarely attack humans. In fact, the attack on Barbara was the first cougar-related death reported in California in 80 years. The chances were much greater for her to have been struck by lightning or bitten by a poisonous snake. Of course, this is no solace for Barbara, who had completed her first ultra, the Cool Canyon Crawl, in March. Both she and the animal were in the wrong place at the wrong time.

Barbara's husband, Pete Schoener, attends the Emigrant Pass ceremony. A 1990 Western States finisher, he is tall and gaunt, with dark, grieving eyes. When Tony and Mo finish, the other ultrarunners and I express our condolences to Pete, now near tears.

No changes are made in the race as a result of this incident, but all runners are briefed on what to do if confronted by a cougar. First, run in groups. Second, if an animal is encountered, face it, take a stance, make eye contact, and "look large." Make noise to confuse and distract the cat. Do not run, crouch or do anything that resembles the behavior of the cougar's normal prey.

A Barbara Schoener Memorial Trust Fund has been established at a bank in Placerville, California, to handle money contributed by Barbara's friends in order to finance construction of a bench at the place where she was killed and to finance the Schoener children's higher education.

Western States is ultrarunning's showcase event, serious business for most of its entrants. Sunmart, a Texas-based chain of truck stops, provides relatively lavish sponsorship, as ultra races go. The pre-race atmosphere is gutcrunching. Some of the athletes, like three-time masters winner, Ray Scannell, try to lighten up the 1994 proceedings by wearing crazy Mohawk haircuts and sequined running shoes.

Actually, the first time I saw someone with a Mohawk at a 100-miler was Don Adolph, of Chicago, Illinois, at Vermont in 1991. Don has white hair and looked quite striking at the time. One of the other runners must have thought so too. He came up to Don at the pre-race briefing and gushed,

"I can't keep my eyes off you. You look wonderful." Don glared at him and the guy went away.

On Friday, the day before the race, I am terrified, scared silly, apprehensive as hell. My stomach hurts and I am lightheaded. Maybe it's the altitude. In the morning, all runners are medically examined, we deliver our drop bags to their collection point, and we pass through race registration where we pick up our goody bags.

The medical check is outside the Squaw Valley Convention Center. Across the street, Jim O'Brien is selling his TrailGators. Gaiters, or spats, are nylon coverings worn over the shoes and ankles. They prevent trail dust and stones from entering a runner's shoes; they also keep socks clean. I am probably the 5,000th person to say, "Jim, I like your gaiters, but the stirrups wear out too quickly."

Jim replies, "We're working on improving stirrup longevity, but in the meantime, you can wrap them with duct tape."

"Thanks, pal; I already discovered that trick." Duct tape — the product with a million uses.

Waiting in line for the medical exam gives me a chance to check out the exotic race T-shirts other runners are wearing — "Finger Lakes Trail Fifties," a New York State event; "Mohican Trail 100", held in Ohio; the "Le Grizz 50 Miler", a Montana ultra. As usual, I'm a walking advertisement wearing my "Uwharrie Trail Adventure Run" shirt. I introduce myself to Hal Winton, Grand Slam class of 1992, who is handing out applications for the Angeles Crest 100 Miler. Bob Holtel is hawking his book, *Soul, Sweat and Survival on the Pacific Crest Trail*, the story of his solo run on the 2,600 mile PCT.

The nurses taking our vital signs are a veteran group. My name, race number, and information from the exam — weight (179 lbs.), blood pressure (110 over 60) and pulse rate (60) — are written on a plastic hospital bracelet which stays on my wrist as long as I remain in the race. Removing the hospital bracelet and handing it to an aid station official is a sign of defeat, indicating withdrawal from competition. God forbid. I've come this far. Someone will have to shoot me before I quit.

Moving inside the Convention Center to register, I am confronted by a jarring scene, a veritable Oriental fleamarket of all kinds of Western States 100 Mile Endurance Run merchandise for sale — water bottles, fanny packs, hats, T-shirts, shorts, sweatshirts, energy bars, pins, rings, key chains, accessories. My apprehension is growing. I don't feel like spending any money. I just want to escape.

At the registration table, I pick up a manila envelope. In it are my race number, 390, and the 25-page Western States Brochure containing the race week agenda, performance rules, crew

45

information, and a list of entrants, among other things. Then I am confronted by a race official who bellows,

"What's your name and where ya from?"

Resenting this invasion of my noise zone, but resisting the urge to reply "I am Tan from the Sun" I inform him, in a subdued voice, "I'm Bob from North Carolina."

"Well, Bob, when you walk down that table over there picking up your stuff give everybody a big smile and a handshake and tell them where you're from."

It's like I'm 12 years old and this is my first day at summer camp. I go along with the act. This is California; being heartily extroverted seems to be mandatory.

As far as gifts for the contestants are concerned, Western States is the polar opposite of Old Dominion. At Western, runners are deluged with two multi-colored shirts, one short and the other long sleeved; a salmon colored polo shirt with the WS logo on the left breast, courtesy of the Ping Golf Equipment Company (Karsten Solheim, a son of the man who owns Ping, is an ultrarunner); a Spenco blister kit; a white hand towel carrying the everpresent logo; a white plastic poncho from Fuji Films; a small bag of Mahatma brown rice; several Kiwi shoe products; a tube of Mentholatum lip balm; a pair of sun glasses; a red Everest sports bag with Western States and SunMart logos to carry all the stuff; and, most exciting of all, a rollette of SQP personal tissue — biodegradable toilet paper.

Since I wear sandals most of the time I don't need the shoe polish, but the other stuff is useful.

Friday afternoon finds everyone stretched out on the lawn behind the Squaw Valley tram building for the "mandatory" race briefing. Up to this point, I have caught only fleeting glimpses of Race Director, Norm Klein, as he has rushed around taking care of business. Now, Norm emerges, microphone in hand, in his starring role as the combination master of ceremonies/*condottiere* of the Western States Endurance Run.

At the briefing, Norm shows off his encyclopedic memory for elite runners' past performances. Calling to the front a dozen of the top male and female athletes and all the foreign entrants, Norm entertains his audience with a recital of their times and places in recent big trail races.

46

Eric Clifton is introduced along with perennial top ten finisher, Dave Scott, 37, from Fremont, California; there's Dow Mattingly, 42, of Walnut Creek, California, who won the men's masters divison last year; Bernd Leupold, 52, of Foresthill, California, a two-time winner of his age group. Lynn O'Malley, 43, of Edmonds, Washington, who usually wins the women's masters division; and Helga Backhaus, 41, of Berlin, Germany, a top European ultrarunner who, with O'Malley, is among the women Norm singles out. An aura of energy, of lift and push, an avidity, surrounds these top ultrarunners as if they are on a quest.

Norm saves this year's race favorites, Tim Twietmeyer and Ann Trason, for last. Tim, 35, an engineer, lives in Auburn so he has the advantage of training on the Western States course. He has finished the race under 24 hours a phenomenal twelve times, won it in 1992, and finished second to course record holder, Tom Johnson, in 1993. This year, Tom is entered in the world 100 kilometer championship held this weekend in Japan, so he isn't defending his Western States title.

Norm has the reputation of being a pretty crusty guy, but he clearly has a soft spot in his heart for Ann Trason, the 33-year-old microbiology lab instructor from Kensington, California, a suburb of San Francisco. He goes on at length about her athletic achievements: five time Western States women's champion and course record holder (18:14:48), five time female ultrarunner of the year; world record holder at 50 miles, 100 km and 100 miles; and course record holder at a dozen trail ultras.

Ann grins and waves at the audience. Her arms are as thin as noodles. As Norm continues speaking, Ann hides her face behind her hair, looking acutely uncomfortable under the shower of praise. She is the High Priestess of Ultrarunning, equally at home on trails, roads, and the track. She was selected for the U.S. team at the world 100 km event, but chose to compete at Western States instead.

Also singled out is Gordy Ainsleigh, the godfather of 100 mile trail running. This is the twentieth anniversay of Gordy's maiden romp on the Western States Trail. Although in those days the course was short, it still boggles the mind to think of tackling Western States without the vast aid station support system in place today.

Norm gives Gordy an opportunity to reminisce about the early days when he was a 27-year-old woodcutter running with the horses for the shear hell of it. It's good to see Gordy getting the recognition he deserves. This praise is a far cry from 1992 when reportedly he was hanging around the Michigan Bluff aid station complaining bitterly that he couldn't even get into the race.

Now a massage therapist, Gordy is a vital component of the brief history of this sport and an inspirational speaker. Tomorrow he will be wearing race number "0". His buddy, Ken "Cowman" Shirk, who in 1976 duplicated Gordy's feat of running the entire distance alone with the horses, will be wearing number "00". A resident of Hawaii, Cowman's universal greeting is "Amooha, I'm a horny guy."

Rick Fisher, the man who has popularized the Tarahumara Indian runners, attends the briefing. A Tarahumara team was supposed to enter Western States and Norm even sent out a pre-race letter asking for contributions to help pay the Indians' expenses. Apparently, Fisher drove all the way from his home in Tucson, Arizona, to Mexico's Copper Canyon where the Tarahumara live, only to discover that their top runners had accepted a more lucrative offer from some Swiss promoters to enter a race in the Alps.

Fisher came to Squaw Valley to apologize for the no-shows and to promise refunds to everyone who gave him money for the Tarahumaras. I was not one of the generous ones. These guys already have numerous advantages over me and most of the other entrants. They are virtually bred to run mountain trails. It is part of their culture. They have a big crew that provides them with customized food and drinks. They run as a team and have their own pacers. They beat me by ten hours over 100 miles.

The briefing finally ends, and Harvey and I return to Tahoe City. I'm in a bad temper. After supper I have difficulty moving my bowels. As I commence the ritual taping, my anger is compounded by the realization that I have forgotten to shave around my nipples. Lights off at 10 PM. The race starts at 5 AM, so we set the alarm for 3:30 which comes quickly. After choking down some breakfast we hit the road for the 15 minute drive to Squaw. It's freezing outside. I'm wearing gloves, a knit cap, and my goretex running suit.

The atmosphere at the start of Western States is like a heavyweight championship fight — one-third out of control hysteria and two-thirds stomach wrenching apprehension. The mob of 380 starters crowds into a narrow sidewalk area under the start banner as the gun goes off. Someone steps on my foot and I curse loudly.

It's dark, cold, and we are faced with a climb of 2,500 feet in 4.5 miles on gravel roads and trails, some very steep. For me this is not the time or place to go berserk and catapault myself to the top, but invariably, every year, some fool wearing neither shirt nor hat and carrying a single water bottle zooms past me at hypersonic speed on his way to the top. This year is no different. Two guys wearing headbands with Japanese lettering on them whizz by.

"Hey," I yell, "Are you trying to commit suicide?"

One turns and gives me a dirty look. His partner glances at me. He's Oriental-American. Oops. I forgot this is California. I'm being politically incorrect.

I don't know why I'm so worked up. Maybe I'm ventilating the pre-race stress. I tell myself to mind my own business and concentrate on pumping my arms which helps propel me to the summit.

Reaching the crest of Emigrant Pass, I pause to face east where dawn is breaking over Lake Tahoe. The water shimmers. The horizon, an inky blue, is crowned with a lustrous pink light that paints the underside of billowing clouds. Snowcapped peaks surround me.

My chest swells as I inhale the crisp morning air at 8,700 feet. An indescribable feeling of joy bursts from within as all the meanness that has been building up inside for the past few days vanishes. Turning to join the stream of runners on the narrow trail leading into the remote Granite Chief Wilderness Area, I reflect that this feeling is what people mean when they talk about the liberating aspect of endurance running.

The pristine Granite Chief Wilderness Area offers splendid vistas of the high country, savage and inviolate. Competitors are strung out in a long line, and passing is difficult on the narrow trail, so I concentrate on safe foot placement on the slippery rocks and mucky stretches.

In 1993, 15 foot snow drifts covered north-facing slopes on this early part of the course making it even more treacherous. Runners were forced to climb up the front side of each drift, run on the slippery top, then jump or slide down the back side. Coping with the extreme conditions exhausted some, forcing them out of the race early.

Two Swedes, Mikael and Robert, are entered in this year's race. Since I'm half Swedish on my mother's side I know a few phrases which I yell at the Swedes when we pass each other.

"*Svenska boyka*," I cry, "Jag talar inta Svenska," "*Tousand tak.*"

"Hallo." They smile quizzically. Mikael, is feeling his oats and disappears down the trail while Robert runs a pace similar to mine and stays within a few minutes of me.

At the 11-mile point, Lyon Ridge is the first major aid station in the race. Crew access is not allowed, but scores of volunteers help us refill our plastic water bottles. I am carrying three bottles filled with water, energy drink, and Mountain Dew, respectively. At this stage of the race and at this altitude, hydration is all important. Runners surge past me on the dirt road leading out of the aid station. I resist the temptation to join them in their uphill charge. "Conserve, conserve, show strength in restraint" is the mantra I keep repeating.

After Lyon Ridge, the trail curves away westward atop Red Star Ridge. Soon we are climbing Cougar Rock, one of the most rugged and beautiful obstacles in the entire race. A photographer perches on the summit of Cougar Rock to record our passing. Throwing out my arms and grinning at him I nearly lose my balance on the steep trail.

At Red Star Ridge aid station, after 16.5 miles and 3-1/2 hours of running, I drink my first can of liquid food supplement. Maintaining my high energy level is vital because the course gets harder. Entering a forested section, I am struck by the immensity of the conifers.

The main problem in the first 30 miles at Western States this year is the dust, especially when a group of runners careers downhill. In the 18 inch deep rut that constitutes the trail, the dust is so thick that I can't see where I am placing my feet. I need coggled eyes in my shoes. Fine grey particles are clogging my lungs, so I pull my red bandana over my nose and mouth.

Denny Hagele, class of 1988, charging up Cougar Rock at Western States.

by Terry Henderson/Photogenix

Breaking out of the forest onto Red Star Ridge, I catch sight of French Meadows Reservoir glittering in the sun. Formed by a dam on the Middle Fork of the American River, French Meadows Reservoir is a major recreation area in this part of the Sierra Nevada Mountains. The descent from Red Star Ridge to the bottom of Duncan Canyon is shadowy and densely timbered. At the 24-mile Duncan Canyon aid station, a runner is being treated for blisters. Apparently, he is looking for an excuse to quit.

"Does this mean I'm out of the race?" he pleads.

"Naw," replies the podiatrist; "This should take care of you." The runner slumps in his chair, depressed at the prospect of continuing.

Climbing out of Duncan Canyon I encounter Grand Slammer Number One, Tom Green. At this stage of the race I'm bursting with enthusiasm, but Tom, a master sand bagger, always quiet and understated, informs me that he is undertrained and feeling lousy. I've heard this before from Tom. Even as I move ahead of him I know he will catch me before the race is over.

Tom Green is one of those remarkable people who successfully complete ultradistance races in excellent times on very low training mileage. In 1986, he trained for his Slam by running on the sidewalks of Columbia, Maryland, and increasing his weekly mileage all the way from 30 to 45.

I suspect that part of Tom's success is due to physiological advantages he enjoys over other people. Looking at him, the first thing you notice after his owlish appearance is his barrel chest. He's a skinny guy otherwise, but I surmise that his lung capacity is greater than normal, which means that his lungs pump more oxygen into his blood than mine do. Modest and religious, Tom is also one of the most courageous runners I have ever met. One story from four years ago will illustrate my point.

The 1990 Massanutten Mountain Massacre 50 Miler in Virginia featured the worst footing of any race I ever entered. I was in my usual position near the back of the pack when I came upon Tom Green standing storklike on one leg at the 10 mile point. His left ankle was weak to begin with, and he had turned it badly on the rocky Massanutten trail.

I felt sorry for Tom at the time because he had a string of Massanutten finishes that he wanted to continue. With the pain that he was in, I didn't see how he could navigate the remaining 40 miles of rocks, roots, and poor footing.

"Sorry Tom," I said as I passed. Dropping out looked like his only choice.

Thirty miles later, Tom caught up with me. He had refused to give up and had limped, then walked, then resumed running enough to make up some of the time he had lost. He finished the race, beating me in the process. Characteristically, Tom did not make a big deal out of it, but I still think this was the most heroic act I have witnessed in a sport where courage is a quality shared by all participants.

Back on the Duncan Canyon Trail, no one has collapsed, but I pass several runners who are hurting. In 1993, on the long ascent from Duncan Canyon to Robinson Flat I discovered a runner lying alongside the trail at the 28 mile mark, completely exhausted. I had seen runners down on the trail before, but I was shocked because it was so early in the race. Running too fast too soon had trashed that fellow.

In 1992, the first year I entered Western States, I arrived at the 30.2 mile Robinson Flat aid station completely fried — dehydrated, sun blasted, light headed. Fortunately, I had enough of my wits left to take my time, eat, drink, and calm down before continuing.

In 1993, on the way to Robinson Flat I was entertained by a fellow runner's story of conflict with his ex-wife over his running. She objected vehemently to all the time he was spending on his long weekend runs so he made a deal with her to keep Sunday afternoons free for joint activities, but evidently that had not satisfied her. They divorced. In 1992, he met a New Jersey woman at Western States who was crewing for someone else; they corresponded, and she moved out to California to live with him. Apparently, telling me his story excited the guy because when we arrived at Robinson Flat, he ran up to his waiting girlfriend and proposed on the spot. She accepted and they fell into an embrace so enthusiastic that aid station personnel told them to knock it off. That was the last I saw of him. Evidently, he dropped out of the race, intent on pursuing other activities.

Today, I arrive at Robinson Flat feeling tired, but in control of myself. Tranquil the rest of the year, this beautiful grassy meadow, called "the Crossroads of the Sierras," is mobbed by cheering crew members. Locating Harvey takes me a few minutes. He hands me fresh drink bottles, a peeled banana, and a can of liquid food supplement. While I am standing there with my hands full, a woman comes up to me holding a camera and asks if I can take her picture when her runner arrives. With bananas and Mountain Dew streaming from my mouth, I inform her, "Madam, I have better things to do, people to meet, and miles to go before I sleep."

The five miles after Robinson Flat descend on dirt roads into Deep Canyon. To the west, Duncan Peak Lookout sits atop a white granite cone. From Duncan Peak one can observe all of central California from the crest of the Sierra in the east to the Coast Range in the west, and from the Sacramento Valley in the north to the San Joaquin Valley in the south.

I'm well fed and hydrated, running easily on cruise control, avoiding glycogen depletion and nausea. In fact, I have eaten so much that nature calls and I begin searching for a likely place to pull off the trail to take a crap. Now is the time to activate the SQP personal tissue.

But, like everything else associated with running 100 miles on trails, defecating in the wild is not as simple as it sounds. As Kathleen Meyer writes in her best selling book, *How to Shit in the Woods:* "Shitting in the woods is an acquired rather than innate skill, a skill honed only by practice, a skill all but lost to the bulk of the population along with the art of making soap, carding wool, and skinning buffalo."

I don't know the first think about skinning buffalo, but I average one dump per hundred mile race so I have honed my technique in previous races, including two on this very trail, and I'm feeling confident. Although it is tempting, I do not follow the childhood rhyme: "In days of old when knights were bold and toilets weren't invented, they left their load along the road and walked off so contented."

Instead, I seek out a private place twenty yards off the trail behind a large pine tree. There, following Kathleen's instructions, I dig a hole. She recommends digging six to eight inches deep, but I don't have a shovel and I don't want to disturb delicate root systems so, with apologies to Ms. Meyer, mine is more like three or four inches in depth. Removing my fanny pack, I pull down my running shorts and squat, making sure that my shoes are out of the line of fire.

A shadow hunched over, I am utterly alone. For a moment, as my bowels empty, I am in touch with my ancient self. Maybe 18,000 years ago I took a shit in this exact same place. Probably the mountains haven't changed that much. I wonder if my antediluvian turds were the same color and smelled the same.

Reluctantly, dragging myself back to the present, I tear off a half dozen squares of Norm's buttwipe, clean myself, deposit the paper in the hole, and kick dirt over the whole mess.

Peeing is another story. At the beginning of my ultra trail racing career when I had to relieve myself, I stepped off the trail and urinated on something — a rock, root, stick or leaf. However, I kept noticing these ten-to fifteen-foot long, dark, wet, squiggly lines in the trail dust. Eventually, when following closely behind another runner, I watched as he slowed down a bit, widened his legs, reached into his running shorts, pulled out his penis, and proceeded to whizz on the run.

What a revelation. I had discovered one of the secrets of trail ultrarunning. Previously, I had been losing precious seconds every time I stopped to take a leak — maybe a total of ten minutes every 100 mile race. Now, after learning how to piss properly, I felt like one of the boys, but I wasn't a truly genuine trail ultrarunner until March 7, 1992, at the Wild Oak 50 near Harrisonburg, Virginia. It was a rainy day and, simultaneously, while I was piddling on the run, chewing on an energy bar and washing it down with Mountain Dew, my nose was dripping, and I farted. That was the ultimate defining moment in my trail running career, if not my entire life.

And, good news for the ladies, feminine funnels are available which fit comfortably between the legs and allow the runner to direct her stream in squiggles in the dust without stopping — just like the men.

Dusty Corners at the 40 mile point at Western States is my favorite aid station of any race because every year the volunteers set up a portable shower. Covering my shoes with plastic they spray me all over with cool water, most refreshing after a long, hot, uphill trek. Stuffing watermelon and cantaloup into my mouth I notice several runners slumped in lawn chairs.

One particular sentence keeps popping up in stories about the successful completion of 100 mile races. The sentence goes something like: "By 70 miles, the enormous quantities of food I had been putting away began to pay off."

Several sentences recur in stories about unsuccessful attempts.

"I had my sights set on finishing in under 24 hours."

"I decided to run the race in my new heel lifts."

"I didn't want to overburden myself so I left my fanny pack at home and only carried a one pint bottle."

"I felt really good at the beginning of the race so I went out a little faster than usual."

Wanting to be a member of the "Enormous Quantities of Food" bunch rather than joining the "A Little Faster Than Usual" group, I stifle the urge to rush out of Dusty Corners: I double check to make sure my drink bottles are full, and I remember to put ice in my cap to cool the blood flowing through my brain. I also take some ice and rub it on the inside of my thighs, my armpits, and on my neck — areas of my body where major arteries run close to the surface. Downing one last cup of Coke, I bid the lawnchair lizards adieu and depart Dusty Corners heading downhill to Last Chance aid station.

Last Chance is a medical check. Stepping on the scale, I tell the volunteers my name and number, and discover I'm only three pounds under my starting weight. Good work, Bob. All my precautions are paying off. My drop bag appears magically from nowhere. I am amazed at the cheerfulness and efficiency of these aid station people. I wish I could bring them all back to North Carolina to help at my races.

Guzzling my liquid food supplement, I notice my fellow Minneapolis native, Mike Erickson, sitting in a chair being exhorted by one of the medical personnel. Mike is a naval aviator, a big, strong blond guy like all good Minnesotans. In 1991, we ran together for many hours at the Vermont 100 Miler and shared a lot of reminiscences of home. I havent seen him for three years so it's like meeting a long lost relative. I charge up to him and start yelling like an idiot.

"Hey, Mike, good buddy, friend of my youth, how's it goin pal, remember me, Bob from Vermont?"

Mike looks pale and not at all well. At my appearance, he bolts out of his chair and takes off down the trail like a wounded lion.

Turning to the physician I ask, "What's Mike's problem?"

"Kidney shutdown. He hasn't peed in three hours."

All of a sudden I feel terrible. Here I am shouting at this guy who, it turns out, has serious medical problems. Renal failure can cause permanent damage to the kidneys and even death. I'm certain that Mike is feeling lousy and my screaming at him made it worse. Now he's heading for the hardest part of the course, inadequately prepared, and I feel it's all my fault.

What a dumb shit I am.

Last Chance is aptly named, situated as it is just before Deadwood Canyon, the first of the three fearful gorges that constitute the major physical challenge at Western States. Deadwood, El Dorado Creek Canyon, and Volcano Canyon come in the middle of the race roughly between 42 and 55 miles and during the heat of the day. Deprived of wind because of their great depth, these ravines become ovens during the day, with temperatures exceeding 100 degrees F.

This remote region is honeycombed with abandoned gold mines. Grizzly Mine, Home Ticket Mine, Beaman Ridge Mine, Rattlesnake Mine, Double O Mine, Elkhorn Mine. In the 1850's, Chinese laborers came with picks and shovels to dig the dark mine shafts and tunnels for their American bosses. They pioneered the trail through the canyons to bring in supplies and carry out the gold.

Appropriately, the trail passes a cemetary before plunging nearly 2,000 feet into Deadwood Canyon. Three miles of switchbacks carry me down the canyon's steeply wooded sides. My ultimate destination on the other side of the gorge is visible, but it looks unattainable. At the bottom, a swinging bridge leaps the swiftly flowing North Fork of the Middle Fork of the American River. My water bottles are nearly empty. On the other side of the bridge, a photographer takes pictures of the runners.

"Hey, friend, can you spare some water?" I ask her.

"Sorry, I've got only enough for myself."

Creep.

The climb out of the canyon is unbelieveably steep. In 1992, about a quarter of the way to the top, I came upon two runners who were lying down by the side of the trail totally incapacitated, unable to continue. Rescue people had brought horses down to carry them out. Apparently, they had salt depletion problems and their legs just collapsed under them.

In 1993, I caught up with two runners, a man and a woman, who seemed to be strong climbers. I fell in behind them like the caboose on a train. The woman was the locomotive. She did the hard work and pulled me out of the canyon.

This year I am alone. A river of sweat is pouring off me. Where is all this fluid coming from? Head down, arms pumping, mind blank, breathing hard, trying to fill my lungs with oxygen, I pass a runner who is babbling incoherently. The climb is neverending. Finally, near the top, I spot a large volcanic outcropping. This is the landmark named Devil's Thumb for the hellish conditions that once existed here for miners; now, runners inherit the site.

The Devil's Thumb aid station looks like a mash unit in a combat zone. Runners are spread out everywhere lying on cots with IV's dripping into their veins. Others slump in lawn chairs oblivious to the activity around them. I feel slightly light headed from the heat and the exertion, but after consuming a can of liquid food supplement, eating a banana, and filling my bottles, I'm ready to go again. Grabbing a handful of pretzels for their salt, I stroll out of the aid station.

"Three-ninety out," I announce to the volunteer checking us as we leave.

More derelict mines litter the trail to El Dorado Canyon: Basin Mine, Sourdough Pit, Pacific Mine. Another delapidated cemetary sleeps at the edge of this gorge. Devil's Thumb, at the 47.8 mile point of the race, is situated at 4,365 feet; the bottom of El Dorado Canyon, at 52.9 miles, lies at 1,700 feet; the trail climbs to an altitude of 3,530 feet at my destination, Michigan Bluff, the 55.7 mile point. That adds up to 2,665 feet of descent and 1,830 feet of climb over a distance of 7.9 miles in the heat of the day — this after already having run half the race.

The narrow trail cuts into the steep sides of the canyon. Fewer trees, less shade, and more exposed rock to absorb the heat of the sun translate into a temperature increase of 10 to 20 degrees over what passes as "normal" in these ravines. I don't know what the temperature is, but again the sweat is literally pouring out of my body.

An aid station has been set up at the bottom of the canyon. Several runners are sitting in lawn chairs. I can tell from the defeated looks on their faces that they have had enough. Some have already removed their ID bracelets. The canyons in this race will kill you. I fill my bottles, eat some melon, and drink two cups of Coke. Someone yells, "Rattlesnake on the trail." I look up in time to see a nice, thick five-foot long specimen slither across the trail.

Lee "El Burro" Schmidt turning on the charm at the Wasatch Front briefing.

by Robert Boeder

Lee Schmidt, standing 10 feet from the snake, jumps up and down, yells, and waves his arms like he is challenging the reptile for possession of that part of the state of California. I am ready to hightail it in the opposite direction, conceding all of California and parts of Nevada to Brother Rattler if that's what he desires. Today, he just slides into the weeds, probably looking for a warm rock to curl up on.

Lee bounds triumphantly uphill; I follow at a more sedate pace. During the 1850's, a great deal of blasting, washing, sluicing, and lumbering took place in this area, completely changing the face of the canyon. Soil to a depth of 150 feet was washed from hundreds of acres exposing the bedrock underneath. This is where Leland Stanford, future U.S. Senator, Governor of California, and benefactor of Stanford University made his fortune. A town called Michigan City once perched on the edge of the canyon but its inhabitants were forced to leave their homes forever when the extensive gold diggings caused the ground to settle, and the town toppled down the mountainside.

In 1859, the present village of Michigan Bluff was constructed, and all the miners moved there. Today, I check into the Michigan Bluff aid station at 7:16 PM. At the same time, the race leaders, Tim Twietmeyer and Ann Trason, are on Auburn Lakes Trail, roughly 30 miles ahead of me. My weight is holding at 175, a few pounds under what it was at the start.

Harvey is waiting for me.

"Way to go, Bob."

He is excited, leaping up and down, offering me all kinds of things to eat and drink. I appreciate his enthusiasm, but I am at the opposite end of the energy scale.

On the long, quiet climb out of El Dorado Canyon, I have sunk into a trancelike state. Transferring quickly from my trail reverie to the hubbub of Michigan Bluff is like emerging from a sealed cocoon into the middle of "76 Trombones" being blown at full blast.

"Cool it, please, Harv."

Harvey has been in this situation himself, so he isn't offended. Calming down, he helps me change shirts, replaces my sun glasses with my regular specs, opens my can of liquid food, gives me my night hat, makes sure I have a flashlight, fills my bottles with energy drink and Mountain Dew, all the while giving me a pep talk about how great I look — everything a good crewman does.

And to his credit, Harv resists the urge to remind me that the word CREW stands for Crabby Runners, Endless Waiting.

"Bob, you're 15 minutes ahead of your best previous time at Western. If you keep it up you can run a personal best."

This is an idea that hasn't occurred to me. Since I PRed at Old Dominion — and since Wasatch will be an automatic PR because it will be my first time finishing that race — I can set twin goals of not only completing the four Grand Slam 100s, but also setting PRs in each of the races. This sounds really tough, but actually my Personal Records aren't all that great, so it is definitely doable.

At the Michigan Bluff aid station I catch up with my Old Dominion pal, Rick Hogan. Rick is being crewed by his Spanish girlfriend, Blanca. Since she is afraid of driving on the gravel mountain roads, Blanca and Harvey have teamed up. She speaks no English and Harv is not exactly fluent in Spanish, but, apparently, they are communicating on a rudimentary level. Rick departs as I arrive.

I spend 11 minutes at Michigan Bluff. On my way out of the aid station, I pass a circus-like scene. One of the runners has brought a very large crew, including her own masseuse. She is lying on the massage table getting a rubdown while her crew members are milling around bumping into each other.

I prefer keeping things simple. My ideal crew size is two — one person to take care of the runner's nutritional and clothing needs and the other to serve as a pacer. Both of these people should be close friends or relatives of the runner, a spouse and a training partner, preferably fellow ultrarunners. Having a dozen people on a crew confuses the runner and detracts from the meditative aspects of the experience. I believe that running 100 miles through these mountains should be a spiritual journey, not a corporate challenge.

Leaving Michigan Bluff the course follows the gravel Gorman Ranch Road through Bird's Valley then proceeds on Chicken Hawk Road. After a few miles, this road forks left toward Volcano Canyon.

In 1994 a new aid station has been set up at this left turn where a ludicrous scene presents itself. Here we are, in the middle of nowhere. One of the volunteers is a Queensize woman energetically blowing a very loud train whistle and bellowing, "GO BABY," at each passing runner. She has been doing this for five hours.

I decide not to stop. *"Une question d'ambiance,"* as they say in Abidjan. Hugging the far side of the road, I sprint past this aid station as fast as I can. "GO BABY" becomes my mantra for the rest of the race. Every time I spot someone I know I yell "GO BABY" at them. This strikes me as hilarious. No one else seems to get the joke. I guess you had to be there....

Descending 800 feet, the trail into Volcano Canyon is narrow and rocky, so steep and eroded in places that a missed step can result in disaster. My feet are moving so fast I'm on the brink of losing control; I'm maintaining balance by extending my arms from my sides; my quads are being pounded. Just past the half-way point in the race, I pray that I survive this section with something left for California Street yet to come.

As always, when in trouble I repeat the Serenity Prayer I learned at Twin Town Treatment Center in St. Paul, Minnesota. "God, grant me the serenity to accept the things I cannot change, the courage to change the things I can, and the wisdom to know the difference." I have recited this prayer several times a day for 11 years, whenever I feel overwhelmed by life. It has never failed me. I always feel better afterwards.

At the bottom of the canyon I hop across Volcano Creek on some conveniently placed rocks. The ascent brings me to the Bath Road aid station where I am overjoyed to find Mike Erickson. Mike has recovered from his kidney problem, is feeling fine, and has been just ahead of me for nearly 20 miles. Jogging along the path beside the Foresthill-Baker Ranch Road, we renew acquaintances. At this point, Mike is stronger than I, and he pulls ahead, anxious to meet his wife, who is crewing for him.

Arriving at the Foresthill aid station, the 62 mile point in the race, is like reaching the New Jerusalem. Hallelujah, brothers and sisters; praise the Lord; we have overcome! The hardest part of the race is behind me.

In 1993, the aid station was decorated like a Hawaiian luau with the volunteers wearing grass skirts. Tonight, I have stumbled into a scene from the Roaring 90's. The men are dressed like refugees from Reno and the women are wearing garters around their thighs. Weird.

When I enter the aid station my name is announced over the loud speaker. As I am being weighed I look around, but there is no sign of Harvey. It's 9 PM, I have been in this race for 16 hours. My feet are killing me, I'm trembling uncontrollably, and my normal sensing system is impaired. All the activity at the aid station is confusing me, and I'm hallucinating on the lights.

It's totally up to me to propel my physical self from Point A to Point B in this race, but I'm emotionally dependent on my crew. Anxiety is so close to the surface that Harvey's momentary absence causes a sinking feeling that feels like someone has stomped on my stomach. Irrational thoughts race through my mind.

"He's had an accident, gotten lost, screwed up somehow. My race is finished, my Grand Slam attempt is kaput, my life is over."

Enter Harvey.

"Where the hell have you been?" I roar.

Wisely, Harv chooses to ignore my tone of voice. He hustles me over to where he has our stuff set up. Rick Hogan has arrived ahead of me. He and Blanca are cuddling. It looks like they have activities in mind that will take Rick out of the race. Foresthill is where Harvey joins me as pacer/trail companion. It is also the place where the "real race" begins at Western States.

Usually, an "out of town" runner, a non-Californian, starts fast and is exhausted by 60 miles, leaving the locals to fight it out for the victory. This year, Alaskan Harry Johnson is first into Foresthill, in just under 10 hours. Tim Twietmeyer is two minutes behind Harry followed by Ann Trason, trailing by nearly a half hour, but clearly biding her time. Harry's race is over and Tim takes the lead.

I'm six hours behind the leaders. Bottles filled, Harvey and I depart leaving Rick and Blanca locked in an embrace. This is why I dont mix sex with ultrarunning. It's too distracting.

The original 19th century Foresthill Chamber of Commerce boosters envisioned their town as a city with a future, so they created a Main Street as wide as Market Street in San Francisco. But after the gold mines played out, everyone moved away. Today, Foresthill's claim to fame is that it has the highest homicide rate in California. Harv and I pass a couple of noisy neon-lit bars that contribute to this statistic before turning left into that section of the course known as California Street.

What's it like to run trails after dark? When night settles in, another world emerges — one where familiarity fades. Strange shadows stalk the trails. Shining eyes peer out of the darkness. A sense of unease pervades; secrets and solitudes fill the night.

Noises carry a long way in the stillness of California Street. Tonight, one of the most common sounds is that of violent retching as someone's stomach rebels against dehydration and the self inflicted violence of running these 100 miles. We never catch whoever is throwing up. He must be running between his bouts of nausea, his stomach muscles sore from all the heaving. We pass a runner sleeping alongside the trail, his pacer, a young woman, sitting silently beside him.

A full moon illuminates the trail, which is mainly downhill with lots of switchbacks and some short but sharp uphills. Four aid stations serve California Street: Dardanelles at the 65.7 mile point, Peachstone (70.7 miles), Ford's Bar (73 miles), and Sandy Bottom (75.8 miles). No crew access is allowed at any of them.

Dardanelles passes uneventfully. Peachstone is Zombieland: several people wrapped in aluminium foil blankets like large baked potatoes sleep on cots while others slump slack-jawed on folding chairs.

Suddenly, between Peachstone and Ford's Bar my flashlight winks out. No warning, no dimming. It just stops working. We are in a forested section where the light of the moon is blocked out by heavy foliage. It's pitch black except for Harvey's light, a $1.99 Walmart special.

I have done something really dumb in breaking the trail ultrarunner's number one rule: don't try anything new on race day. Earlier in the week I purchased a $20.00 light-weight flashlight with four double A batteries that promised to produce an especially bright light. I never used it in a race before. The thing lasted two hours.

For some reason, I didn't buy the Walmart flashlights that worked so well at Old Dominion. Often in the past, I have used a lithium-powered miner's headlamp as my 100-mile night running light, and it has always served me well. I brought it along with me to Western States, but at the last minute decided to leave it in my bag and carry the new light which is a bit less cumbersome. I'm now paying for my stupidity. I'm not carrying a backup light. The two of us are running solely by the light of the moon and Harvey's Walmart cheapo.

Hurrying through the night, a panic ulcer shifts from side to side in my stomach. I'm in the lead holding the light. I turn it off on the moonlit stretches but I'm forced to turn it back on in the woods where we risk injury if we try to move blindly along the rocky twisting path. My mind races. If our one remaining light fails, we will have to stop and wait for the next runner and use his light as best we can. How long will we have to wait? Will we be able to keep up with the next runner? Will he be too slow?

My pace slackens at night, so I have a small margin of error as far as cutoff times are concerned. I haven't memorized the cutoff times for the California Street aid stations, but I think they close around 2 AM. Pressing the button of my Timex Indiglo watch reveals the time, 1 AM.

We finally reach Ford's Bar where one of the volunteers provides us with four double A's. Bless you, my brother. You have saved our backsides. We're back in business, at least temporarily. A lot of these aid station people have been helping at Western States for years and do a fantastic job of anticipating runners' needs.

We're following old water ditches and miners paths built during the Gold Rush. The ditches were part of a system constructed to provide water for a hydro-electric turbine that supplied Foresthill with electricity.

In the faint moonlight the trail is barely visible. Our flashlights are turned off. Sandy Bottom aid station lies just ahead of us when something moves in the shadows. The hair on my neck stands on end. Cougars prowl at night. Flicked on, my light reveals two law enforcement people — probably Forest Service Rangers — on horseback. Leather creaks as they shift in their saddles.

I'm angry. These mounties scared the crap out of me. They must have heard us coming. Why didn't they say something to warn us? And what the hell are they doing here in the first place? Spying? I remain silent as we pass. Harvey, Mr. Friendly, as usual, speaks to the riders.

"How ya doin?"

I want to shout, "Shut up, Harv. These idiots scared the shit out of me," but I keep quiet. The riders don't reply.

We reach Sandy Bottom. The name describes the locale — the canyon of the Middle Fork of the American River. Last year I nearly collided with a donkey standing in the middle of the aid station. The volunteers used the animal to carry in their supplies. This year I am ready for the donkey, but, unfortunately, it isn't here. Apparently, they brought their supplies in on motorcycles.

I'm in a hurry now, caught up in the excitement of arriving at the Rucky Chucky river crossing aid station, two miles from Sandy Bottom.

"It's an amazing place," I inform Harv, "Like a set for a Hollywood movie."

A few days earlier on our way to Tahoe City, we drove to Cool, California, turned left on Sliger Mine Road, parked our vehicle when the road became too rough, and walked down to the river. Across the boulder-strewn stream all was quiet — a sandy area, a few trees and some day campers. On Western States weekend, the place is transformed into a small city. Noisy generators provide electricity for the banks of lamps that floodlight the scene.

A gravel road transports us the last mile to Rucky Chucky where we check in at 2:30 AM. After five hours in the darkness, Harv and I are dazzled by the energy of the place. After filling our bottles, I am anxious to cross, so we make our way to the river. The spillway on the dam upstream has been closed to cut down on the volume of water bursting along the stream bed.

Oversized pickup trucks are backed up to either side of the river's edge, and a steel cable stretches between them. Plunging into the icy water, we seize hold of the cable and make our way hand over hand across the river which is over 100 feet wide at this point. A volunteer in a wet suit stands at the half way point to warn us of large boulders on the bottom and to catch any runner who loses his grip and is swept downstream. The water touches my crotch. Actually, this is soothing because, due to excessive flatulence, I have developed a bad case of burning butthole.

Last year another runner joined me on the crossing, and, for some unknown reason he started jerking the cable up and down. The water was higher than this year, which forced me to carry my water belt and my spare bottle, so my grip on the cable wasn't as sure as it should be and I nearly let go. Completely losing control,

I began screaming "Hold the fucking cable steady, stop shaking the goddamn cable."

Cursing a blue streak, I strode out of the water. At the aid station, after I apologized to the volunteers for my bad language, one of them looked me in the eye and said,

"You're going to make it."

"You're damn right," I shouted.

This was a revelation. I realized that getting angry pumped me up, brought adrenalin into my system and energized me. Looking around the aid station, I noticed the usual number of half dead bodies — people whose races had ended prematurely. I felt contempt for them.

"Rage rage," I felt like yelling, "Explode, go berserk if you want to finish."

The two mile climb out of the canyon at Rucky Chucky to the next aid station at Green Gate is on a steep gravel road. My shoes are wet from the river, but they dry quickly. Some runners change shoes a half dozen times during the race, but I like to keep it simple so I wear the same pair the entire 100 miles.

Green Gate, the 80-mile point, is decorated festively with a red carpet and Christmas lights. In 1993, my pacer, a local guy in his 60's who I had just met, told me that Green Gate was at the 82-mile point. My psychological dependence on him was such that even though I knew Green Gate was 80 miles into the race, I believed him when he said 82. Eighteen miles remaining sounded better than 20, so in my mind I rationalized his mistake by thinking that maybe the Green Gate aid station had changed location from the previous year. Imagining that I had a half hour cushion on the cutoff time for the next aid station, I took it easy over the ensuing five miles.

This fellow was a veteran volunteer at Western States. I don't know what caused him to mislead me, but personnel at the 85 mile aid station, Auburn Lake Trails, warned me that I was only a few minutes ahead of the absolute cutoff time of 7 AM. If I wanted to stay in the race, I would have to exert myself for the next five miles. Realizing what had happened and stung by my own mental laziness, I reached down and found the energy to run as hard as I had ever run in my life. Unable to keep up with me, my erstwhile pacer dropped out, and I finished the '93 race with 16 minutes to spare.

This year I have a two hour time cushion, but my whole body is sore. It's the hour before dawn. The air temperature has cooled to its lowest point of the night, and my body is begging for sleep. Walking behind me, Harvey notices that I am faltering and encourages me.

"You can still get that PR, Bob. Pick up your pace, swing your arms more."

It seems as if we keep retracing the same ground as the trail winds endlessly in and out of identical tributary stream ravines. Passing the spot where the cougar jumped Barbara Schoener, tears burst from my eyes. I offer a small prayer: "Barbara, may you soar with the eagles that glide over this canyon."

Dawn breaks at the Auburn Lake Trails aid station where I find Tom Green. Tom is sitting in a chair with that thousand-mile stare on his face. I try to sneak past, but he spies me and reluctantly arouses himself. When Tom dodges in front of me I yell, "I'm still going to beat you, buddy."

As Harv and I meander another five miles in and out of the ravines, we keep hearing snatches of rock and roll oldies. What's Little Richard doing up this early in the morning? Are Bill Haley and the Comets appearing at the American River this weekend? The music is coming from the Brown's Ravine aid station at 90 miles, where, every year, the famous Buffalo Chips Running Club of Sacramento turns up the volume on its sound system to welcome Western States runners.

Steps lead up to the aid station, where the Browns Ravine official greeter, a guy dressed up as the devil, offers us a beer. Herb Tanimoto of Cool who finished the Slam in 1987, is working here. I introduce myself and we hurriedly shake hands. The sun is up now, and I'm beginning to feel better.

It's amazing how the body reacts to the sun's comings and goings. Two hours ago, when it was still dark, I was sore all over and could barely crawl. Now, having progressed an additional six miles, the sun comes up and all of a sudden I feel rejuvenated. It's not anything I have eaten or drunk. My body is responding to daylight, like the heliotropic reaction in plants.

From Brown's Ravine the trail carries us downhill to the American River where we join a road which leads us to a limestone quarry. A long trail ascent from the riverside brings us to the

Highway 49 aid station at 93.5 miles. I feel dynamic. Only 6.5 miles to go — a little more than 10 kilometers. I can do that. It's 7:38 AM. Two more hours of running will bring me to the finish in time to break my personal Western States record of 28:46:21 set in 1992. Two hours to run 10 kilometers, a distance which I usually race in around 42 minutes.

For the home stretch, I change into my favorite gray with black lettering "Uwharrie Trail Adventure Run" t-shirt. At the finish line, I want to look good and advertise my race at the same time.

Highway 49 connects Auburn with Cool then heads south to Placerville. Crossing the highway, I find myself following two guys with the initials S.L.U.T.S. printed on the backside of their running shorts. After staying silent for ten minutes my curiosity gets the better of me.

"All right,I give up. What does 'sluts' stand for?"

"St. Louis Ultra Trail Society" is the response.

What a let down. I was hoping for something juicy like "Stay Loose Under The Sheets" or "Slimy Lowdown Ugly Testical Swallowers."

Scooting past the "St. Louis Slutsters," Harvey and I enter a typical central California landscape — scattered trees and tall yellowing grass. It reminds me of an African savanna. Any second I expect to spot a giraffe grazing among the trees or come upon a pride of lions lazing in the morning sun.

The trail is flat. A wave of energy sweeps over me. My feral instincts aroused, I pick up speed. Soon I am flying across this make believe African countryside like a gazelle: knees high, head up, chest expanded, legs stretched out. Not even pausing at the Pointed Rocks aid station, I glance back to see if Harv is keeping up. He's still there, but he's working hard.

"Gosh, Bob, what's gotten into you?"

"I smell the barn, Harv. GO BABY."

At 96.8 miles we charge into the No Hands Bridge aid station. In 1912, when No Hands Bridge was completed, spanning the American River just past the confluence of the Middle and North Forks, it was the longest concrete arch railroad bridge in the world. It's still a stellar piece of engineering, but now it's used only by hikers and runners. Last year the women helping out at the aid station asked me to leave because they said I smelled like a polecat. This year I entertain them with an exhuberant knock-knock joke.

"Knock knock."

"Who's there?"

"Wa."

"Wa whooooo."

After crossing No Hands Bridge, we travel a mile and a half along the abandoned railroad bed that parallels the American River. A final hard climb deposits us at Robie Point aid station on the outskirts of Auburn. A group of crew members and volunteers celebrates each runner at Robie Point. Only one mile to the finish line, in front of the stands at the Placer High School stadium. I've passed a bunch of people during the last four miles.

I haven't looked at my watch since Highway 49. Now I check the time: 9:15 AM. Great. I've got 30 minutes to travel this one last mile in order to set a new PR. Just past the aid station, the street we are on, Robie Drive, changes from dirt to pavement. Two steps onto the pavement, a pain knifes through my right foot. It feels like I've been stabbed. Our progress comes to an abrupt halt.

"Hey, Harv. Wow, this smarts. Somethings wrong with my foot. I can't walk."

A large blister under the two smallest toes on my right foot has broken and I am reduced from running strongly to barely hobbling. My Personal Record is in jeopardy. All the people I recently passed start catching up with me. The last uphill on Channing Steet ends. Half a mile to go. Barely moving, I limp down Marvin Street, then Lubeck, and finally Finley Street.

Finally, we reach the Placer High School football field. Sobbing, an enormous tidal wave of relief washes over me. As I circle the track, Paul Meyer, the announcer in the booth on top of the stadium, proclaims my name and ultrarunning accomplishments. Say what you will about "Western States hype," this is a sweet moment. Waving my cap at the cheering crowd, I manage to sprint the last 100 yards before crossing under the finish banner.

Norm Klein is waiting for me. I give him a big hug as he places the Western States finisher's medallion around my neck. The exhilaration I feel at the end of this race is one hundred times better than any drug high I ever experienced in the bad old days. My time is 28:31:53, good for 185th place out of 249 finishers, and a Western States personal best by 15 minutes.

My feet are killing me, so after the nurses take my pulse and blood pressure I totter over to the podiatrists who have set up their operation on the football field next to the massage tables. In addition to the blisters beneath my toes, other blisters cover the sides of my heels and sting the bottoms of my feet; none of them are deep enough to cause extensive tissue damage. Nevertheless, I'm not happy with the condition of my feet and decide to get rid of the expensive trail shoes I have worn at both Old Dominion and Western States.

I don't see Tim Twietmeyer, who won the race in 16:51:01, but Ann Trason, who came in second overall in 17:37:51 is visiting with friends nearby. We shake hands and I congratulate her. Grand Slammer Joe Schlereth, finishes third overall and first male master runner in 17:51:06.

Harv and I drive to our motel where we shower. I ice my swollen hands and ankles; then we return to Placer High School for lunch in the school cafeteria and the awards ceremony, conducted in the Earl Crabbe Gym. Western States has the distinction of having the longest awards ceremony of any running event in the history of mankind.

Various volunteers are recognized with Friend of the Trail awards; Gordy Ansleigh, who completed the race in 23:50:07, is feted again; Tim and Ann receive the Wendell Robie and Drucilla Barner Cups, respectively, plus Western States Cougar bronze sculptures plus age group awards. (Overall winners should not be eligible for age group recognition, but that's the way it's done here.)

Wendell Robie was the Auburn banker who in 1955 founded the Western States (Tevis Cup) 100 Miles in One Day Horse Ride and also provided the inspiration for the Western States Endurance Run. Dru Barner was the first female winner of the Tevis Cup and the lady who helped create the Western States Trail Foundation; she also inspired Gordy and the other early Western States runners.

Tim's victory is his second in the last three years. He has completed a phenomenal 13 Western States 100's, all in under 24 hours. Bill Finkbeiner, also of Auburn, receives his "1000 Miles, Ten Days" buckle for completing his 10th Western States 100, all under 24 hours. Helga Backhaus, 41, is third female overall and first master in 21:20.

After the top competitors are honored, the other finishers are called up to receive their buckles, starting with the slowest — those completing the race in 29 hours or more. I'm sitting in the gym balcony with Rick, Blanca, and Harvey. Blanca is warm, energetic and very happy that Rick finished the race. Despite my exhaustion, I am attracted to her.

When the 28-hour finishers are called to collect their buckles, I stand up but nearly collapse because my right leg has gone to sleep. After massaging my leg to get the blood flowing again, I limp down the stairs to the gym floor passing Bernie Leupold and Alfred Bogenhuber, the two top guys in my 50-59 year age group; they finished 12th and 16th overall, in 20:17 and 21:03, respectively. Their achievements overwhelm me as do those of Harold Carling, 60, and Ray Piva, 67, whose times are 22:08 and 23:29. Ray is the oldest male ever to receive the silver buckle for completing Western States in under 24 hours.

Most of the Grand Slam Hopefuls of 1994 who ran with me at Old Dominion make it through Western States. Dixie Madsen finishes in 29 hours, Lee Schmidt in 28:17, Cindie Grunt in 28:15, Burgess Harmer in 25:45, Steve Schiller in 25:26, Larry Ochsendorf in 23:31.

Maurice Beaulieu was forced to drop out at the Rucky Chucky River Crossing. MoBo left Foresthill two minutes before I did, but some salt tablets he ate made him sick, and he couldn't continue past the river crossing.

Other 1994 Grand Slam hopefuls who join us at Western States after completing the Vermont 100 are Ken Burge, Terry Smith, Doug McKeever, Tom O'Connell, Mark Bodamer, and Paul Akiyama.

I'm so pleased with my brass buckle that I don't stop grinning until I am back at the motel and tucked in bed. After sleeping 16 hours Harvey and I rouse ourselves. It's Monday, 27 June. We eat a big breakfast at Sweet Pea's Restaurant in Auburn then drive back to San Francisco where we spend some time in the Stinson Beach area around Muir Woods and the Dipsea Trail. On Tuesday, we fly back to North Carolina. As we arrive at Charlotte Airport, my feet and ankles itch furiously, a sign that injured tissues are healing. I scratch happily.

Tom Green, Class of 1986, the first Grand Slammer.

UltraRunning, Vol. 6 No 6, November, 1986

The Trail of the Western States Endurance Run

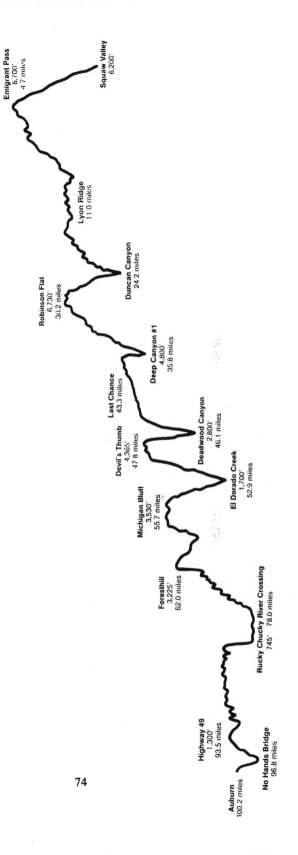

Emigrant Pass
6,700'
47 miles

Squaw Valley
6,200'

Lyon Ridge
11.0 miles

Robinson Flat
6,730'
30.2 miles

Duncan Canyon
24.2 miles

Last Chance
43.3 miles

Deep Canyon #1
4,800'
35.8 miles

Devil's Thumb
4,365'
47.8 miles

Deadwood Canyon
2,800'
46.1 miles

Michigan Bluff
3,530'
55.7 miles

El Dorado Creek
1,700'
52.9 miles

Foresthill
3,225'
62.0 miles

Rucky Chucky River Crossing
745' 78.0 miles

Highway 49
1,300'
93.5 miles

No Hands Bridge
96.8 miles

Auburn
100.2 miles

Suzi Thibeault (L) and Lou Peyton (R), class of 1989, collect their Western States buckles.

Chapter 4

The Leadville Trail 100.

The Race Across the Sky. There Are No Shortcuts.
Leadville, Colorado (Elevation: 10,430 ft. The highest incorporated city in the USA.) 19-20 August, 1994. San Isobel National Forest. Weather Forecast: Unpredictable, but should be partly cloudy with daytime temperatures in the 70's and nighttime temps in the 30's.

July 1. My birthday. Happy 52, Bob. Frankly, I'm surprised that I have been able to finish two hundred mile races in the space of three weeks. The effort at Old Dominion did not hurt my race at Western and may even have enhanced my fitness. The only negative effect from OD was tender areas on the sides of my heels which carried over and were aggravated at Western, turning into serious blisters. The main ill effect upon completing WS has been increased tiredness, so I take a week off from running. Mentally, I'm in good shape and looking forward to Leadville in seven weeks.

My blisters have healed, and the dead skin is pealing off my feet. I am throwing away the Adidas Response Trail shoes and am going back to my old faithful Nike Air Pegasus. Rockport Shoe Company, the Leadville 100 sponsor, is encouraging runners to try its footwear during the race, but I'm not going to experiment with anything that will jeopardise my chances of finishing. I'm staying with the Nikes.

During the seven week interim between Western States and Leadville my job takes me to Southern Africa for two weeks. This is an exciting journey since the last time I visited Malawi and South Africa was in 1982.

I am unable to run during the four days of flying time, but otherwise I manage to work out for an hour each day. These are always hilly runs. I run up and down the hills in Zomba, Malawi, where my daughter was born. I get in two tough workouts running around the Union Buildings in Pretoria, the executive seat of the South African government. In a remote part of the Eastern Transvaal I park my rental car in a picnic area then run up and down Skurweberg Pass, pretending I'm leading the Comrades Marathon. South Africans driving by honk and give me the thumbs up sign.

July is winter in the Southern Hemisphere, so the weather is mild and I don't sweat much during my runs. I also don't get a chance to do any long runs. Although I don't overeat at supper or breakfast, and just eat fruit for lunch, when I return home I'm five pounds over my normal weight. I attribute some of that to fluid retention. During my first few runs in hot and humid North Carolina, I drop a couple of pounds, but I'm struggling to return to the fitness level I enjoyed before Old Dominion. The main problem is that my legs feel like cement. They don't hurt, I just have no leg speed. I can run up hills with no trouble, but I've lost that springy feeling.

This impression that I am out of shape introduces a whiff of anxiety into my life, an odor of fear. I'm worried, my confidence is shaky, and my legs are weak. Maybe this whole Grand Slam business is too much for me. After all, it is unknown territory. Still, I had hoped I would feel better than this.

Maybe the age factor is kicking in. It is not something I normally dwell on. I prefer to ignore the fact that I am 52, but it is a reality. The majority of successful Slammers have been in their 30's and 40's. Only six runners in their 50's have accomplished the Slam (three in their 60's), so who am I to think I can do it? I'm just an ordinary trail runner when you come right down to it. I have no special talent for this sport. The anxiety is devouring me.

25 July. I am back working out on my machines. This exercise is important. I have taken a month off the Nordic Track and the rowing machine, and it's time to get back into my old habit of nightly workouts on one or the other machine. Hopefully, this will restore life to my legs. I'm going to try a long run this Saturday and see what happens. Maybe the Africa trip has nothing to do with how my legs feel, and it is just residual fatigue from back to back 100 milers. If that's the case, I should be ready to go by 20-21 August.

On my trip to Africa, I read Bob Holtel's book, *Soul, Sweat and Survival on the Pacific Crest Trail*, about his solo south-north run which took him three summers to complete. This was a fabulous achievement similar to David Horton's record-breaking Applachian Trail run a few summers ago. What I am trying to accomplish, finishing four 100-milers in one summer, pales in comparison with what these two guys did.

All I have to do is wind myself up for an all-out effort, four times during a 14-week period, but they ran rugged trails day after day while sleeping outdoors much of the time and worrying about food and water supplies. Their accomplishments required enormous logistics skills, mental and physical discipline which I greatly admire.

I like the quote Holtel uses to begin one of his chapters. It is something Gordy Ainsleigh once said, "Life is just too easy. Society is so cushioned that we have no opportunity for struggle. People are bred to struggle. We need to express that or else be incomplete."

The struggle to survive is one of the aspects of living in Africa that always appealed to me. In countries like Zambia and Malawi, every day is an adventure. I enjoy ultras for the same reason. Although these races are an artificial concoction and runners can drop out whenever they want and return quickly to the air-conditioned world of push button entertainment, at least a 100 mile trail race gives us the chance to wage a physical battle for something, even if it is just a belt buckle and a finisher's T-shirt.

27 July. I'm looking forward to Leadville, "The Race Across the Sky." Even though my legs still feel dead, my depression was only temporary, and I have rediscovered my positive attitude. My flight reservations have been made although the ticket price was not a welcome piece of news. I have also made motel reservations and I've gotten in touch with my nephew, Mike Boeder, who will act as my combination crew and pacer.

Mike lives in Boulder Colorado, where he maintains his fitness riding his bike in the summer and skiing in the winter. In May I sent him some suggestions for a summer running program to get him ready for Leadville. From the sound of it, he hasn't followed my instructions to the letter, but at least he's running for two hours at a time and he has gotten used to running with a water bottle. I'm counting on Mike's youth and enthusiasm to provide good company during the latter stages of the race.

On Saturday, 30 July, I have a scare. While trimming bushes in my back yard, I feel a sharp pain on my left wrist. Throwing off my glove I discover that I've been stung by something, probably a wasp, although I never saw it. The area around the sting quickly swells, and by the next day there is extensive swelling of my hand and wrist.

Sunday evening I go over to Carl Barshinger's house and he gives me some Benadryl. I take half a dozen 50 mg tablets, one every couple of hours Sunday night and Monday morning, hoping that the antihistamine will knock out the sting and reduce the swelling. Instead, by Monday morning I'm knocked out and feeling woozy from the Benadryl. The swelling has advanced to my elbow and my hand is so puffed up I can't make a fist. I look like Popeye the Sailor Man — "toot toot" — but I feel lousy.

Finally, Monday afternoon I go to my neighborhood Doc-in-a-box who tells me to stop taking the Benadryl and to keep my hand elevated above my heart so the fluids in my arm drain out. I should be all right in a few days. After paying $46.00 for that advice, I return home and go to bed with my arm propped up. Sure enough, the next day the swelling has gone down and I feel better. Better yet, when I go out for my noontime run the old zip has returned to my legs.

Apparently, taking a day off and resting was what I needed to make my dead legs come alive. The wasp sting was a blessing in disguise. I was pushing too hard to regain my pre-Old Dominion fitness level. Originally, I thought this seven week interim would be an excellent opportunity to rest and recover from Old Dominion and Western States so that I would be sharp for Leadville and Wasatch, but actually it contains a minefield of dangers designed to blow up my quest to finish the Big Four.

7-8 August. Two weekends before Leadville. The weather is beautiful in Fayetteville, low humidity with daytime temps in the 70's. On Saturday I do 17 miles and leave the machines alone; on Sunday I run 11 and work out on my Nordic Track in the evening. On Monday my body feels tired, but, at the same time, my legs feel strong. It's time to begin tapering, so I will run my normal week but only work out on my machines every other evening.

I'm already thinking ahead to Wasatch. I've made my airline reservations and will start looking for a motel. Altitude is a problem at Wasatch so I need to find a place over 7,000 feet. It looks like I will be doing the race without a crew or pacer. Last week I received trail maps and a seven page booklet of instructions. Apparently, race management has been stung by years of criticism of the poor trail markings because this booklet contains practically a step-by-step description of the entire 100 mile course. But I'm getting ahead of myself. First, there's Leadville.

Reading past articles in *Ultrarunning* about the Leadville Trail 100 is not encouraging. In 1985, O.R. Petersen wrote one called "Losing at Leadville" recounting how —coughing, shivering, and vomiting and with his lungs filling with fluid — he almost died from dehydration and hypothermia. Peter Gagarin's 1991 article was entitled simply, "Calling it Quits." Leadville is the race where 1990 Grand Slammer Dick Collins' streak of 800 races at all distances without a DNF came to a crashing halt. Jeff Hagen compared running Leadville to "running Western States with a sock stuffed in your mouth."

The town of Leadville sits on a high plateau watered by the Arkansas River and overlooked by the tallest mountains in Colorado, Mt. Elbert (14,433 feet), and its towering neighbor, Mt. Massive (14,421 ft). Above 11,000 feet, high alpine terrain greets hikers while vegetation on the lower elevations consists of aspen groves mixed with a variety of conifers. Wild flowers border the trails.

Historians know Leadville for the fabulous riches of its gold and silver mines and for its famous ladies, like Baby Doe and the Unsinkable Molly Brown. Race co-director, Merilee O'Neal, follows in that fine tradition of commanding women. She watches over all the details that contribute to the success of this event, and she coordinates the hundreds of volunteers who make Leadville unique. What sets this race apart from the other 100 milers is the townspeople, who are friendly, down-to-earth, and wholeheartedly behind the race. Local medical and radio people provide support, different clubs and civic groups staff the aid stations, and even the district Forest Service office helps out. Proceeds from the race fund numerous charitable causes in Leadville.

The main challenges at Leadville are the altitude and the wild weather that can descend at a moment's notice on the high points of the course, Hope Pass (12,600 ft.) and Sugar Loaf Pass (11,200 ft.).

In 1993, preparing to run the race for the first time, I researched the question of acclimatizing to vigorous exercise at high elevations and discovered several theories on the subject.

Instructions from the race directors recommended spending three or four weeks training at altitude before the race. This approach wasn't feasible since I couldn't arrange that much time off from work. Veteran Leadville runners like Bud Martin of Charlotte, North Carolina, advised me that the race could be successfully completed either within 24 hours of arrival at high altitude or after staying above 9,000 feet for at least 72 hours.

Gene Thibault, an experienced mountain climber and trail ultrarunner and the husband of Grand Slammer, Suzi Thibault, suggested a formula whereby the body requires 24 hours to adjust to every 1000 feet of altitude over 5,000 feet. Once I arrived in Leadville, residents told me that regardless of how long one stays there, the well-trained runner will only perform at 80% of his sea level capability. This last bit of information was not encouraging, but I decided to try the Thibault method.

Since the difference between 5,000 and 12,600 is 7,600 feet I arranged to arrive in Leadville eight days before the race. The first two mornings I awoke with mild headaches, which quickly went away. I also experienced shortness of breath each morning. After two days, these symptoms went away and I felt fine.

In 1993, on my first full day in the mountains, I hiked to the top of Hope Pass and walked down without much difficulty. On my second day, I ran the Leadville 10K road race. The course was out and back on a dirt road, slightly downhill the first half and uphill the second. I ran my age — 51 minutes and change — which was an all time personal worst for 10K, but I consoled myself with these reflections: I was only running at 80 % of my usual strength, I finished second in my age group, and I beat half the people entered in the race.

On my third day in Leadville, in 1993, I climbed Mt. Elbert, surviving a violent rain and hail storm on the way up and reaching the top in brilliant sunshine. This exhilarating ramble gave me confidence in my ability to finish the race, which I did in 29:04, 99th place out of 134 finishers (296 started).

Based on this experience, in 1994 I decide to cut my acclimatization time in half from eight days down to four so I fly to

Denver on the Tuesday before race day, rent a car at the airport, and drive west to Leadville, where I've booked a room at the Little Tundra Motel, four miles outside of town on Highway 91 North. This is where I stayed last year. The Little Tundra is a small place with only a dozen units. Highway noise can be a problem, and the floor in my room slants alarmingly; however, I have a kitchenette, so I can cook my own meals. The owners of the motel, Oda and Larry Wilson, and their family were so nice to me last year that I wanted to come back to Leadville just to visit them.

On Wednesday morning I wake up with a low grade headache, but it soon disappears. After breakfast, I drive into town. Leadville is a grubby place, down at the heels except for a few blocks of stores in the downtown business district on Harrison Avenue. Free Spirit Travel Agency, Merrilee O'Neal's business, where all entrants go to register is on Harrison Avenue across the street from where the race starts. Merrilee is there and greets me warmly.

"Welcome to Cloud City, Bob. Sign in so we know where you're staying." Merrilee tells me that this year 357 runners from 36 states and 4 foreign countries have come to race. Women's course record holder Ann Trason (20:38:51) is here, but the men's record holder, Jim O'Brien (17:55:57), couldn't come. The Tarahumara Indians are here and will probably break Jim's record.

Merrilee's co-race director, Ken Chlouber, is also in the store. Ken is 55 and looks great. A former pit boss at Climax molybdenum mine, Ken is the dynamic personality behind the race. Like H.A.W. Tabor, a Leadville businessman who became Lieutenant Governor of Colorado in 1878, Ken is a politician representing Lake County in the Colorado state legislature. But unlike Tabor, Ken has finished the Leadville Trail 100 nine times, and this year is going for his 10th buckle. Last year he ran 25:42 for a PR. I congratulate Ken on this achievement and ask what his plans are for this year.

"This year I want to go under 25 hours to earn one of our extra large buckles, the ones people point at and say, 'Look, isn't that big?'" he laughs.

Lots of running paraphernalia is for sale at Free Spirit — shorts, sweat shirts, hats, T-shirts with sayings like "Shut Up And Train" and "Just do the work, bud."

Charles Raper, a physician from Knoxville, Tennessee, is at the store. I recognize Charles because we ran together at David

Horton's Mountain Masochist 50 Miler in Lynchburg, Virginia. He is one of the few runners from the southeast at Leadville this year. Charles is worried about how far he will get on Saturday. For the last two weeks, he has been dealing with a tendon problem in one of his big toes. Usually, toes intrude on runners' lives when their nails blacken, die, and fall off. Having something go wrong with a tendon is unusual. This problem will make it tough for Charles to run in the mountains because the toes press hard against the front of the shoe on the downhills and there are lots of roots and stones to kick or trip over. I wish Charles good luck, but privately I'm wondering how long he will last in the race.

Next, I drive over to the May Queen Campground at the western end of Turquoise Lake, the location of the first aid station in the race. From there I hike the course along the Colorado Trail and Hagerman Pass Road to the top of Sugar Loaf Pass and return, a total of about eight miles. I feel all right so long as I stick to hiking, but when I try to run, I quickly become light headed.

Sitting on the shore of Turquoise Lake eating my lunch, I admire the scenery. A hundred years ago, the Sugar Loaf and May Queen silver mines in this area made people rich. The lake is relatively new, formed by a stream dammed to provide power to the nearby town. It's a lovely place encircled by mountains and pine forests. The water is too cold for swimming, but boating, trout fishing, and camping facilities are available.

Highway 24 follows the Arkansas River and the tracks of the Denver and Rio Grande Western Railroad south out of Leadville. As I drive on 24 through the settlement of Balltown, the old stagecoach road is visible on the far side of the river. At the Clear Creek Reservoir, I turn right on Clear Creek Road and, 12 miles down the gravel, pull over at the Hope Pass Trailhead.

Two couples from Minnesota have just returned from hiking the trail. We spend a few minutes talking. On Saturday the men will be running and their wives will be crewing for them. One of the guys entered in 1993, but dropped out at Winfield, the half way point. This race draws lots of Minnesotans — 19 have entered this year, the third largest state contingent after Colorado (113) and California (49).

Strapping on my running belt and water bottles, I commence my climb up Hope Pass. At the top, the views from both sides of the

Pass are spectacular, full of mountains and lakes with Leadville in the distance.

The way down is steep. The sun batters the back of my neck. I'm forced to go fast. By the time I reach the road, my quads have turned to jelly and my calves feel like lead. Maybe that's why they call it Leadville.

Returning to the motel, I find a phone message waiting from my nephew Mike. He'll be here on Friday evening. After fixing supper, I go over my legs with a hand-held Pollenex Power Massager. Normally, I leave the worrying to others, but I'm concerned about my fitness. The stiffness in my legs bothers me, and I wonder if I have given myself enough time to acclimatize. These are all problems of my own making. I go to sleep wondering if I'm subconsciously trying to sabotage my own Grand Slam plans.

On Thursday, I return to Turquoise Lake and run/walk 13 miles of the course along the lakeshore from the Tabor Boat Ramp and Campground to May Queen and back. My legs are still sore, but at least I don't get dizzy this time. Last year I rested on the Thursday before raceday. In retrospect, climbing both Sugar Loaf and Hope Pass the first full day at altitude was a stupid thing to do, especially so close to the start of the race.

In the afternoon, I drive over to the town of Frisco to buy three six-packs of Ensure Plus and a couple of Garrity Life-Lite flashlights at Wal Mart. I don't want to repeat my Western States flashlight mistake. In the evening, I attend the pre-race supper and pick up my race packet at the 6th Street Gym. My number is 99, my place of finish in last year's race.

The supper isn't very good. The pasta sticks together and the lettuce is soggy. But the Gym is worth the visit. It's an ancient building with a basketball court surrounded on three sides by a spectator's balcony. The supper tables and chairs are spread out on the court. Special Leadville 100 clothing is for sale and the free beer is flowing. Neither interests me. Leadville is the only 100 miler that provides alcohol to anyone involved in the race. Because of my past I don't like being around anyone who is drinking. I stay out of bars and I don't permit alcohol in my house. I realize that the town has a reputation for two fisted drinking and that Ken and Merrilee are trying to create a hometown party atmosphere, but I think booze is out of place at an event like this where good health is celebrated.

After standing in line for my food, I'm sitting across the table from a guy wearing a Navy Seals T-shirt. It turns out he is retired from the Navy and lives in Juneau, Alaska, where he directs the State Highway Patrol's physical fitness program. On Saturday, he's going to crew and pace Harry Johnson of Anchorage. Harry is an outstanding athlete, capable of winning here, but not if he repeats his Western States performance where he went out too fast and had to drop out at the river crossing.

This year's race motto, "There Are No Shortcuts" is emblazoned everywhere, on T-shirts, banners, and posters. Detours and deadends aren't mentioned. The official poster carries the race description: "100 miles over some of the world's most unforgiving back country. It's an extreme test of courage and determination and a tribute to how far the human spirit can go."

Friday morning I wake up to rainy weather. Something else to be anxious about. June and July in Leadville were completely dry, but for the past two weeks it has rained every day. Back in the 6th Street Gym for the medical check and final briefing, I weight in at an all time pre-100 mile race high of 179 lbs. My rationalization for the flabbiness is that at this altitude I'm probably retaining fluids. At this point I can't do anything about it. My blood pressure is fine — 116/66, but my pulse is a little high at 70.

The briefing is a good show, with Ken Chlouber in fine form. Ken always tells the story of the Leadville 100, how the Climax molybdenum mine shut down in the early 1980's leaving the town in the lurch with a 40% unemployment rate, and how he decided to promote tourism by organizing a 100-mile trail race. The first race in 1983 drew 45 starters. Ten finished. With Western States as its guide, Leadville has become one of the top ultra endurance events in the US, reflected this year by the presence of ESPN2 and Free Wheelin Films camera crews.

Ken lays on the "We're all family at Leadville" sentimentality as thick as maple syrup. Normally, platitudes make my backside itch, but Ken's sincerity is genuine and since he has finished this race nine times, he can say anything he likes.

One of the annual highlights of the Leadville briefing is presentation of the Jackass Award to the runner who has done the stupidest thing in the previous year's race. One year Mike Monahan of Laguna Beach, California, won because his wife locked him out of his vehicle when he wanted to drop out. In 1993, another Californian, Errol Jones, was singled out for refusing to drink the water at the '92 race leading to his DNF due to dehydration. This year, two awards are given out — one to a woman whose crew neglected to bring dry shoes for the river crossing thus forcing her to drop out, and the other for Handsome Harry Deupree of Mustang, Oklahoma, for finishing last in 1993 with only 15 seconds to spare.

Don Kardong, of *Runner's World* magazine, is the featured speaker at the briefing. Don tells the story of his experience at the 1976 Olympic Games at Montreal, where he was the third member of the U.S. marathon team along with the more famous Bill Rogers and Frank Shorter. With a mile to go, Don was in third place, the bronze medal position. As he entered the Olympic Stadium, another runner passed him and he wound up in fourth place, causing Kardong to miss an Olympic medal by three seconds. Not medaling was disappointing, but just being on the Olympic team was still a wonderful achievement and when he returned to his hometown of Spokane, Washington, he expected to be idolized. But he discovered that the average person had no idea what he had done or where he'd been. Don's point was that what we do as distance runners we do for ourselves, for our own satisfaction, not for any popular acclaim or financial reward because these don't exist in the world of trail ultrarunning.

Don's speech puts me in a reflective mood. This is the summer of the baseball strike. Team owners and players are squabbling over money. Owners want to put a cap on player salaries. The players react by refusing to play. All these people are paid more money than is decent. No such problems in the sport of ultrarunning. This is also the summer of the Rwandan civil war, of crises in Haiti and Cuba, and of the O.J. Simpson tragedy. As I deliver my drop bags to the front yard of the Lake County Courthouse on Friday afternoon, it seems these events are taking place on another planet.

I'm getting nervous. I have that queasy feeling in the pit of my stomach, a premonition of impending doom. Friday evening I'm eating supper alone at a restaurant near the motel. World class 100 kilometer masters runner Sue Ellen Trapp and her daughter Kristina are waiting for a table. Kristina is only 23. Last year she entered Leadville. It was her first race ever at any distance and she DNFed. This year she is back for her second attempt. Her main sport is tennis, but apparently she wants to prove herself as a runner. She looks pale, nearly overcome with anxiety.

I speak to her: "Kristina, I feel the same way you look. This linguine with cream sauce isn't going down very easily."

She replies, "I feel like I'm going to throw chunks."

Late Friday night my combination crew, pacer, and nephew, Mike Boeder, arrives with some friends of his, a young couple thinking of joining the Peace Corps. Since I served as a volunteer teacher in the African country of Malawi in the mid-1960's, they want to talk to me about my experiences. It's after midnight by the time our conversation is over and they leave. That gives me and Mike just a few hours of sleep before our 3 AM wakeup call.

The race starts at 4 AM in downtown Leadville at the corner of West 6th and Harrison Avenue. We arrive a few minutes early in order to check in with race officials and so I can stretch my muscles. Standing in the street with 316 other pumped up starters under the glare of television camera lights, I feel as though a giant barroom brawl is about to break out.

Thankfully, the shotgun is fired before the fight starts, and the crowd slowly begins to move. Not 100 yards down 6th Street, the runner right in front of me, Aaron Goldman, of Los Alamos, New Mexico, steps in a pothole severely turning his ankle. Leaping aside, I avoid the same calamity. Looking back, I see Goldman limping over to the sidewalk clutching his leg. This is where luck enters the Grand Slam picture. That could easily have been me. In the excitement of a race start, nobody pays any attention to foot placement.

After a few minutes, the pavement ends and we begin a five-mile stretch of gravel road that includes a short but nasty climb up a powerline before we are delivered to the trail that circles past Tabor Boat Ramp and around the north side of Turquoise Lake. A breeze off the lake cools the morning air, and the whole scene is lighted by a fabulous full moon on our left. On this seven miles of narrow rocky trail, most runners stay in single file, our flashlight beams bouncing up and down seeking out the heels of the people in front of us.

Everyone is full of energy and we tend, unwisely, to race through this section. When a slow person or someone without much experience finds himself at the head of a long string of runners, people try to sprint past in order to gain a few minutes. The idea is to pick up my feet and run with my knees high to avoid tripping over the rocks.

The sun rises near the end of this section. Just before we reach the May Queen campground, I find myself right behind Dixie Madsen. Suddenly, Dixie trips and pitches headlong into the rocks. I stop briefly to ask if she is all right. Of course, she says she's okay, but I can tell that one hurt.

The May Queen aid station is inside an Army-style GP Medium tent. I have covered the 13.5 miles in 2 hours, 35 minutes. Already, the leaders, Johnny Sandoval of Gypsum, Colorado, and Ann Trason, are an hour ahead of me. Most of the runners move quickly through the musty-smelling tent grabbing a coke or a banana, before emerging into the light of early morning. Outside, Mike is waiting for me with a liquid meal in a can. He walks with me the half mile up Sugarloaf Dam Road to the Colorado Trail.

Before joining the trail, the course passes through a hikers' rendezvous area and crosses one of the many creeks feeding Turquoise Lake. The Colorado Trail surface, mainly dirt covered with pine needles, is very runnable, but this stretch is a one mile uphill; most of the competitors are speed walking. Reaching Hagerman Pass Road, we take a right and break into a run, but the road surface is rocky and uneven — no fun to run on.

Off to the right across a valley, power lines snake along the mountainside. After about a mile, we turn left onto a powerline road that claws its way up Sugarloaf Mountain. Keith Stegall of Mt. Elbert Films is at the intersection with his video camera. Keith has videotaped the race for years, and everybody greets him as we go by.

Sugarloaf Pass tops out at 11,000 feet. The downhill is steep and loaded with switchbacks — a real quad burner, but at this point in the race, we are all still relatively fresh and no one cares. It's a sunny morning and I'm feeling limitless; there is nowhere else I'd rather be. Reaching the paved Leadville Golf Course Road, we turn right and before long arrive at the Fish Hatchery Aid Station, the 23.5 mile point. This aid station doubles as a medical check point where we are weighed and our physical condition is assessed.

I'm suspicious of medical checks, viewing them more as places where my Grand Slam plans can be ambushed than as brief but necessary examinations. So when the doc asks how I feel, I'm not going to call attention to myself with some flippant reply like, "At one with the universe," even if that's the way I feel. I just look him in the eye and say, "Fine, okay," and he lets me go.

Departing the Fish Hatchery, runners turn eastward and follow the paved road for a short distance before taking a right on the flat dirt Halfmoon Road. Looking at a course map, one would think that this is a place for fast running where time can be made up, but the road hasn't been graded in a while. It's like an uneven washboard, and I can't fit my stride into the ruts because the distance between them is not constant.

Crews are only allowed to drive as far as the tree line on Halfmoon Road, the point where the trees of the San Isobel National Forest start. When I get there, Mike is nowhere to be found. Fortunately, I have planned for this situation and a drop bag awaits me at the Halfmoon Aid Station, another two miles down the road. There are times when meeting your crew is absolutely essential, but this isn't one of them.

At Halfmoon, 30.5 miles into the race, I consume a Mountain Dew and a can of Ensure Plus then move on down the road. Last year, I threw up at this aid station after drinking two cans of the liquid meal — sixteen ounces — instead of my usual single eight ounce can. My stomach couldn't digest that much fluid, so it just came up the same way it went down. I felt much better afterwards. The volunteers at Halfmoon had seen this happen before. They told me to eat a banana to settle my stomach and everything turned out fine.

This year I'm feeling fine. Back on the road, I catch up with Dot Helling, from Montpelier, Vermont. We've never met before, but we've both contributed articles to *Ultrarunning*, so each of us knows something about the other. One of the best things about running 100 milers is these chance meetings along the trail where friendships are quickly established on the basis of mutual respect and shared interests. Dot has excellent form and is running very smoothly at this point in the race.

After turning off the road and onto the Colorado Trail, Dot and I are joined by Lee Schmidt and later by Melissa Lee-Sobal of Leadville. Melissa regales us with a description of her snowshoe race to the top of Mt. Elbert the previous winter. Today, we're running along the eastern flank of Colorado's highest peak in fine weather, the four of us chattering like chipmunks.

The conduct of our small group contrasts sharply with what is happening at the front of the race. Johnny Sandoval has dropped back, and two of the Tarahumara, Juan Herrera and Martimano Cervantes, have caught up with Ann Trason, but the Indians are acting strange. In their culture, women cook, clean, and mop up after the kids; a Tarahumara woman wouldn't dream of competing on an equal basis with the men, especially in trail running.

The Indians are reacting to Ann's presence in the lead by staging their version of a ghetto challenge act, speeding up and passing Ann then stopping and starring at her as she goes by. This behavior is unsettling and kind of spooky, but Ann has been insulted by some of the best male trail runners in California, so it's nothing new. In fact, she turns it to her advantage by getting angry and becoming more determined than ever to run hard and beat whoever is acting like a jerk.

Toward the end of the Colorado Trail section, we pass the place where in 1993 I shouted "bayete" as I passed South African runner Sipho Mkhalipi. "Bayete" is the Zulu equivalent of "banzai." Sipho turned up at the 1993 Leadville race with a story of having arrived destitute in New York from the South African city of Durban; he begged money to buy a bus ticket to Vail then hitchhiked over to Leadville. Sipho was an engaging fellow with a big grin and, being suckers for a sob story, members of the ultrarunning community opened their hearts to him, providing him with free room and board, waiving the $100.00 entry fee into the race, and even collecting $500.00 in spending money for him.

Sipho told everyone that he was a 2:16 marathoner and top ten gold medal finisher at the Comrades Marathon; he added that his goal was to win Leadville to attract financial sponsors. To my eyes, though, he didn't have the physique of a top marathoner. For one thing, his legs were too short. And his brand new running shoes and expensive running suit somehow didn't fit the image of impoverishment he was projecting.

Sipho's race day performance didn't fit the hype either, as he dropped out at Twin Lakes, the 40 mile point. Nevertheless, he took a curtain call at the awards ceremony and waved happily at the applauding runners and crew members as he accepted an envelope stuffed with cash from Ken Chlouber.

That should have been the end of the story, but the imaginative Sipho was a man with a plan. Upon returning to Durban, he announced that he had won the Leadville 100 in the record-breaking time of 13 hours and 45 minutes. Claiming his first place prize was $150,000, he appeared on South African television, brandishing an impresssive winner's trophy. Suspicious South African sports reporters soon unmasked Sipho, revealing his tale of trickery.

No South Africans show up in 1994. Only the Tarahumara, who arrive at the Twin Lakes Fire House aid station three hours ahead of me.

When I trot in, Mike is there apologizing all over himself for missing me at Halfmoon. I tell him not to worry about it and step on the scale for the second medical check of the race. Down two pounds. Nothing serious. Not knowing what the weather will be like at the top of Hope Pass, I change into a long sleeved shirt and tie my goretex running jacket to my fanny pack.

From Twin Lakes (9,200 feet), the course crosses Highway 82 and heads south, through the half dozen streams that comprise Lake Creek. Some runners waste a lot of time here making a big fuss about changing shoes and putting on dry socks. I just splash right through knowing that my shoes and socks will dry in 15 minutes. People worry about wet shoes causing blisters, but that only happens when one is running in the rain and shoes stay wet for hours.

Passing a group of parked vehicles and horse trailers, I begin my ascent of Hope Pass. Yesterday, the horse trailers were used to transport the llamas that carry supplies to the aid station near the top of Hope Pass. The trail follows Little Willis Gulch and I pass by several abandoned mine sites. I'm alone at this point: breathing deeply, climbing steadily, pumping my arms, and taking frequent swallows of energy drink mixed with Mountain Dew. I feel strong. It's a gorgeous sunny day. Last year during this climb, I passed a number of runners who had stepped off the trail to rest. The beaten looks on their faces told me they would not be among the finishers.

Martyn Greaves, the 1988 Grand Slammer from England, argues that the first 40 miles of this race to Twin Lakes are relatively easy so people tend to go out too hard leaving nothing in reserve for the double climb and descent of Hope Pass between 40 and 60 miles, considered by many to be the toughest 20 miles in the Grand Slam series.

Roughly half way to the top, a chill of excitement seizes my body as Ann Trason and her pacer/husband, Carl Anderson, fly past me on their way back to Twin Lakes. Ann is in the lead and they are moving fast. I'm thrilled to wish Ann well and briefly to merge my emotion with the feelings of this couple as they make their joint effort to win the Leadvile Trail 100.

Last year, I was near the top of Hope Pass when the leader at the time, another female runner, Christine Gibbons of Hackensack, New Jersey, passed me on her return trip to Twin Lakes. I recall being astonished at how fresh and unfazed Christine looked. She went on to finish fourth overall in 20:55. Today, Ann is well ahead of Christine's time at this point and on record pace.

Twenty minutes later, the second place runner, a young Tarahumara, goes by me with a big grin on his face. Who said these people are shy and hide their emotions? I give him the thumbs up and yell "bueno, bueno." The thought occurs to me that if this guy is having such a wonderful time at the 57-mile point, Ann might be in trouble.

Passing more runners on their way down, I emerge from the tree line and sight Hope Pass, the highest point of the race at 12,600 feet. The trail is dug into the ground as it switches back and forth on its way to the top. The flora in this area is delicate, but it's hard to avoid trampling the vegetation when several runners converge on the same place and someone has to vacate the trail to let the faster runners by.

The Hope Pass aid station is on my left, several hundred yards below the pass itself. On Friday, llamas carried supplies up to this place and the animals now graze peacefully nearby. Several runners are sitting in the aid station, but I don't want to waste time here, so I grab a cup of chicken noodle soup, thank the volunteers, and resume my climb.

Reaching the top of the pass is another thrill. Pausing briefly to take in the spectacular views of Twin Lakes and Leadville in the distance, I joke with a photographer.

"Hard way to make a living," I tell her.

"At least I'm getting paid for being up here," she replies.

Last year, there were snow flurries at the top. This year, the weather is perfect. I don't even need my jacket.

The trail downhill is treacherously steep in places. I have no choice but to go fast and pray that I wont trip and dive face first into the rocks. Crossing the boulder field is dicey. One misstep and my leg slips into a crack between two boulders shattering my ankle.

Finally, the descent of Sheep Gulch is over and I arrive at Clear Creek Road. Mike is there with a fresh water bottle. I tell him there is no need to drive the two miles to Winfield, the half way point. "Just wait here for me to come back."

As I turn right on Clear Creek Road somebody yells, "Hey Bob."

Startled, I look around. It's Eric Clifton being crewed by his wife, Shelby. "Hey, Eric, how's it goin?" I'm shocked to be so close to Eric — only four miles separate us, about an hour of running. Normally, Eric is four or five hours ahead of me at this point in a 100 miler.

"Not so good," he replies. "I only got out here on Thursday."

That explains it. Eric is struggling with the altitude. Thin air cuts even the top runners down to size.

I don't enjoy this two mile run into the ghost town of Winfield. The road is dusty, congested with traffic, and the surface isn't good for running. The gravel hurts my feet. A lot of Leadville runners drop out at Winfield. They cant face the thought of turning right around and climbing Hope Pass again. At this point, I'm not doing a whole lot of thinking. I'm just doing.

Entering Winfield, I manage to throttle up to a saunter past some abandoned miner's log cabins, turn left, cross a bridge, then make another left into the campground, where the aid tents are set up. Another medical check. It's 4:30 in the afternoon. I've been on the move for 12-1/2 hours. My weight is three pounds down, so I'm doing fine with the hydration.

A young boy, around 10 years old, asks me if I want anything. My initial reaction is to tell him to get out of my way, I'm busy, but I dont want to discourage him, so I ask for a Mountain Dew. My right foot is killing me. I'm looking for a place to sit down. The kid comes back; "We dont have any Mountain Dew. Here's a Sprite." "Okay, thanks buddy." The Sprite tastes better than I thought it would.

This is the first time I have sat down all day. Taking off my shoe is tricky because when I pull on my heel, my Achilles tendon stretches, causing a severe cramp in a muscle near my butt. Maybe it's some sort of nerve malfunction. The sudden pain of the cramp causes me to cry out; my face contorts. An older woman, one of the volunteers, has been watching me. She turns away. Cursing under my breath, I stretch out my leg and massage the cramping muscle.

The shoe and the sock are off now. I'm trying to wrestle a blister patch out of its package. There are two large blisters, one on either side of my right heel. I'm losing patience with this operation, real quick. The blister patches are on, but they don't look like they'll stay in place for long. I don't care. I just want to get out of here. Puting my sock and shoe back on, I leave the tent. The older lady looks relieved that I'm departing.

The idea now is to retrace my steps back to Leadville. Clear Creek Road is full of unhappy runners. In an attempt at levity I yell at a couple of the ones I recognize:

"Suck it up, Eddie" and "Hard to the finish, Tom." No response from either of them. Looks like they've had it. Half way up Hope Pass, Dixie Madsen passes me on her way to Winfield. It's already past 5 PM, so obviously she will not make the 6 PM cutoff. I remember her fall at May Queen and just say "Hey" as we pass.

Leaving the tree line behind, I find myself leading a group of five climbers. In years past, I would have stepped off the trail and given the lead to someone else, but today I'm mentally strong and feel that I am climbing well. No one is in a hurry to zip past me, so I play locomotive pulling the group steadily up the steep switchbacks. A surprising number of runners are on their way down to Winfield and DNFs. Most of them get out of our way and wish us well.

At the summit, the six of us shake hands and briefly exchange congratulations. "Way to go," "Good climb." It's a moment of elation. The hardest part of the race is over.

At the bottom of the descent from Hope Pass, Harry Deupree catches up with me in the flat grassy section west of Twin Lakes Reservoir. Harry is going for his tenth Leadville finish this year. Even though he has an injured knee his power walk is so strong that I have to run to keep up with him.

"Are there many ultrarunners in Oklahoma, Harry?"

94

"Just a few, Bob. Maybe you know Tulsa Ross Waltzer."

"No, I don't know him, but I know Mike Robertson who's stationed at Fort Sill."

"Yeah, earlier in the summer I ran into Mike during a training run on Mount Scott near Lawton. Nice fella and he's gotta fine family."

I follow Harry back to Twin Lakes, the 60 mile point in the race. A lot of runners drop out here. It's a convenient place to call it quits: it's usually getting dark and no one enjoys running through the night; crews are there to meet runners, so a ride in a nice warm car back to the motel is at their fingertips; and some of the runners stay in motels in Twin Lakes, so, for them, a shower, hot meal, and soft mattress are just around the corner.

In 1993, descending Hope Pass I hooked up with two young guys from Minnesota. I told them the hard part of the race was over and they had 14 hours to negotiate 40 miles, but they wanted no more of the Leadville trail and dropped out at Twin Lakes. They were depressed because they weren't going to finish in under 25 hours, but I was pumped up because I knew that if I just kept moving I would finish.

Both of these guys had attractive, athletic looking wives waiting at Twin Lakes to encourage them. All that was waiting for me at the aid station was my drop bag containing some clean clothes and a can of Ensure Plus. Sitting in the Twin Lakes Fire House that night, I fought a primitive urge to slip into the darkness and kidnap the wives of the two quitters — my prize for finishing Leadville. Their husbands would be banished from the ranks of ultrarunners to Minot, North Dakota, where they would spend their remaining years running in circles around the junior high school track. The women would join me, like the female elk that go with the dominant male elk who wins the big horn butting fights during mating season.

This year I arrive at Twin Lakes at 8:30 PM just as it is getting dark. No elk graze here, but Mike meets me, and I change shirts again and pick up the goretex runing pants that I might need if the night turns cold. The Colorado Trail awaits. I'm confident that I can finish the race.

My plan is to conserve energy for the Sugarloaf Pass climb while at the same time moving fast enough to finish under 29 hours to keep my PR streak going.

Checking out of the Twin Lakes aid station, I'm surprised to catch up with Martyn Greaves.

"What're you doin here, Martyn? You're usually miles ahead of me at this point."

"I know. I'm nursing an injury I got at Hardrock last month."

Martyn works for an insurance company, and every summer his employer sends him to the U.S. on business, so he takes advantage of the situation and enters several 100 mile races. Jogging along the trail, we overtake Harry Deupree who cuts a ghostly figure dressed in white tights and a white, long-sleeved shirt.

The nine miles to Halfmoon take three hours. My night walking pace is slow, but Martyn lags behind. He must really be hurting. I'm wearing a knit cap and polypro gloves along with three layers on top — long sleeved polypro next to my skin, a short-sleeved cotton T-shirt in the middle and my goretex jacket on the outside. With these and my running shorts and goretex pants, I'm warm enough. I'm staying hydrated and my sugar level is fine, so my spirits are not sagging. Thankfully, it's not freezing cold tonight — yet.

At Halfmoon, the 70 mile point, Mike joins me for the long trek to the finish. It's all road to the Fish Hatchery aid station (76.5 miles) where we check in at 1:30 AM. This is the final medical check. I sit down for the second time in 21 hours so the doc can measure my blood pressure and check my pulse. Considering the altitude and the effort I have expended, my pulse is fine at 96; BP is near normal at 110 over 66.

Lee Schmidt is falling asleep in the chair next to me. I wonder if his race is over. As we leave the Fish Hatchery I tell Mike, "Prepare yourself for a hard climb to the top of Sugarloaf Pass."

Several pairs of runners pass us on the paved road. Turning left, we cross a stream then pick up a dirt road that shadows power lines up the mountain. Sparks fly as the lines hiss and snap in the darkness.

Last year, I climbed this dirt road under the worst race conditions I had ever experienced: snow, rain, sleet, below freezing temperatures, and gale force winds punished exhausted runners throughout the night. Tonight the moon is full and the weather is fine. Mike and I climb slowly but steadily up the southwest side of Sugarloaf. Pausing twice to urinate, we begin picking off the guys who went by us on the road.

This is the place where earlier, in the evening, Juan Herrera made his move on Ann Trason, passed her, and went on to win the race by 36 minutes, but it is not a good spot for mere mortals to step on the gas. At the 80 mile point of the Leadville Trail 100, the steep struggle up Sugarloaf at 2:30 AM, with its endless switchbacks and false summits qualifies as a religious experience.

Post-summit, the 1200-foot descent to May Queen and Turquoise Lake is no place for weakened quads. After re-joining the Colorado Trail, Lee Schmidt catches us. This guy is amazing.

"Lee, You've come back from the dead so many times I'm changing your nickname from 'El Burro' to 'Lazarus.' I thought you fell asleep at Fish Hatchery."
"Ya, I was pretty tired, but a coupla cups of coffee and some soup picked me up. I feel fine now."

As Lee lopes into the darkness, I wonder if I'll see him again. Sure enough, he's sitting inside the tent at May Queen, grey-faced, looking like he's been rode hard and put away wet. I try to sneak past him, hoping he's too exhausted to be paying attention. Last year I jumped a lot of half-frozen runners at May Queen who were trying to recover from the effects of the blizzard conditions on Sugarloaf.

This year it's a gorgeous moonlit night. Thirteen miles left; 5:20 AM. Mike and I hook up with a group hiking the north shore of Lake Turquoise. Soon, Martyn Greaves catches up. I congratulate Martyn for his recuperative powers. And next, who passes us but — you guessed it — Lee Schmidt, running hard. Who can figure this guy?

6 AM. The sky brightens. To my right, across the lake on the top of Sugarloaf, I can see two tiny beams of light bouncing up and down, a runner and his pacer with their flashlights, making haste for May Queen. The aid station closes at 6:30. They aren't going to make it, but they are still trying. Ultrarunners. Too stubborn to admit defeat.

There is a toilet at the Tabor Boat Ramp campground. I tell Mike to use it if he has to, but I'm not stopping. Last year I wasted ten minutes here waiting for my pacer to finish his toilet business;

then I finished the race in 29:04. Had I not sat dumbly for ten minutes I would have broken 29 hours. It was my own fault. John, my pacer, a local fellow who didn't know me but volunteered to run the last 30 miles with me out of the goodness of his heart, didn't ask me to wait for him, I just did it without thinking of the time I would lose. That happens at the end of a 100 miler. Thinking becomes such a burden that the runner depends on whomever he is with to make all the decisions. Plus, I was grateful to John for helping me over Sugarloaf. At one point in the dark, I wandered off course, but he realized what had happened and brought me back.

This year I am determined not to repeat the same mistake. If Mike has to take a dump, he can do it then catch up with me. My goal is to finish the race under 29:04.

Leaving the lakeshore path, we step onto a gravel road. I try jogging occasionally, but my feet are too sore. In addition, I'm uncomfortable in all of these clothes so, I take off my jacket and pants and tuck them into the ties on my fanny pack. Walking as strongly as I can, we catch up to Gary Zicker, from Boulder City, Nevada, who I recognize from Western States. Gary is not happy. He spent over an hour at May Queen and is dragging himself to the finish, crawling along at a snail's pace. He still retains his pride though and doesn't want to be passed, so he picks up his walking speed enough to stay with us.

We turn right on the path alongside the Denver and Rio Grande Railroad tracks. The surface is sandy, softer than the gravel road and easier on my aching feet. I slip it into a slightly higher gear for a hundred yards or so, but I can feel the exhaustion deep in my bones so I return to walking.

Soon we're on the final gravel road to the finish. This is Leadville's final insult: three miles, mostly uphill, of gravel - not the ordinary brand, but a unique variety of extra-large stones imported specially for this race. This stuff is killing my feet, but other runners don't seem to mind. Rich Shear from Wellsville, New York, who I met at Old Dominion, trots by along with Al Binder of Evergreen, Colorado, who is finishing his eleventh Leadville 100. What kind of shoes are these guys wearing?

Finally we're back in Leadville. At the 6th Street corner, a bunch of guys cheer for us. I know one of them, South Dakotan Larry Simonsen. Earlier in the summer, Larry entered the Trans-America race. He even led the race for a couple of days but had to drop out because of an injury. He had a great time running across the country and wants to try again in 1995.

Mike and I are on the home stretch, walking the final uphill to the finish, at the corner of 6th and Harrison. Glancing at my watch, I discover that I'm not going to break 29:04. A small disappointment that I'm too tired to care about.

A red carpet in the middle of the street covers the final fifteen feet of the Leadville Trail 100 course. My name and hometown are announced, I charge up the carpet and break the finish tape in 29:20:38, 135th out of 156 finishers. Merrilee hangs a medal around my neck and gives me a big hug. I receive a manly handshake from Ken Chlouber, who has completed his tenth Leadville: 1000 miles across the Rockies. Twenty roundtrips of Hope Pass. Amazing.

Searching for Mike, I find him on the sidewalk. Giving him a hug, I thank him for being there for me. I'm footsore, dog tired, but euphoric as we drive back to the motel.

At noon, two hours after the end of the race, everyone gathers at the gym for the awards ceremony. All finishers receive a hooded sweatshirt with their names and times screened on the sleeve. The female finishers are given gold and silver necklaces. All runners completing the course in less than 25 hours are awarded gold and silver belt buckles. Those reaching the finish line in less than 30 hours get silver buckles.

Four of the top five finishers are Tarahumaras. Twenty-five-year-old Juan Herrera sets a new course record of 17:30:42. Ann Trason comes in second in 18:06:24, breaking her course record by 2-1/2 hours, putting her fourth on the Leadville Trail 100 all time finishers list.

Dot Helling becomes the first Vermonter ever to complete Leadville by finishing in 28:58:20. Harry Deupree records a time of 28:21:45. Martyn Greaves crosses the finish line in 29:04:44.

I am reminded of what Larry Robbins wrote in a 1987 article in *UltraRunning*, "The keys to success at Leadville are: preparation, planning, luck, pace, concentration, food and fluids, luck, staying injury-free, prayers, desire, and luck."

Dixie Madsen and Steve Schiller, two of the Grand Slam hopefuls who started the series with me at Old Dominion, ran out of luck at Leadville and did not finish. Twelve of us are headed for Wasatch. If you want to rope the wind, you've got to believe.

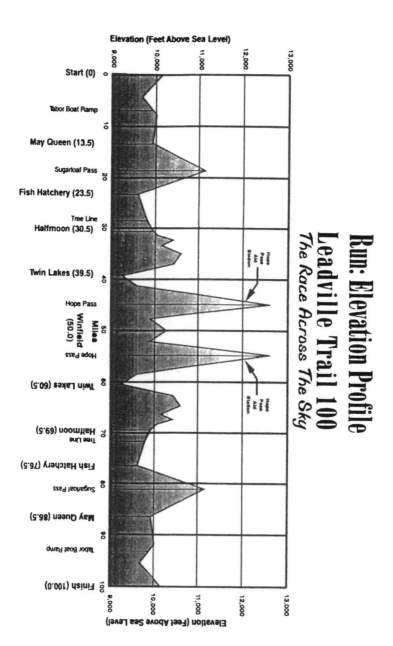

Run: Elevation Profile
Leadville Trail 100
The Race Across The Sky

Chapter 5

The Wasatch Front 100 Mile Endurance Run.

100 miles of heaven and hell.

Salt Lake City, Utah, 10-11 September, 1994, Wasatch National Forest. Weather forecast: temperatures in the '80's during the day. Low humidity. Strong winds. Chance of PM thunder storms.

26 August. After returning to North Carolina from Colorado, I take four days off then start running again on Thursday. One hundred miles in the Rockies gave me blisters on the outer corner of each heel; and the bottoms of my feet are sore. But that's all. My feet heal in a few days. After the race I rubbed my legs with Sports Creme and went over them with my massage machine and they feel fine.

One new post-race discomfort is soreness just under my rib cage on the right side. Strangely, it doesn't hurt when I breathe hard while running, only when I am sitting down resting. I may have pulled a muscle while taking deep breaths in the mountains.

My training plan is to work fairly hard next week, running six miles every day and working on my machines in the evenings then stop the machines after Labor Day and taper off the week of the race.

I have a USAir frequent flyer ticket I'm using to fly to Los Angeles. From there I will fly Delta to Salt Lake City for $121 round trip then rent a car in Salt Lake. I called Rick Gates, a 1990 Grand Slammer from Salt Lake City, for advice about the race. Rick will be going for his 10th Wasatch finish this year. He is manager of Cliff Lodge at Snowbird ski resort, and I will be staying there while I'm in Utah.

Ten-time Wasatch finisher, Rick Gates, class of 1990

by Robert Boeder

It looks like I will be doing the race alone since no one has volunteered to crew for me, and I haven't really asked. I don't know anyone in Utah, and it's hard for people in the east to pay for their own ticket to fly out just to help me.

It's been a great way to spend the summer. Flying around the country to four of America's most beautiful vacation destinations, renting cars, staying in posh motels, meeting old friends and making new ones, food and drink provided on a fully catered weekend, plenty of exercise and fresh air. Who could ask for more?

The classic quote about the Wasatch 100 comes from a 1986 *UltraRunning* article by Red Fisher: "The race continued as I hammered up the trail, passing rocks and trees as if they were standing still."

Since this is my first time at Wasatch I am trying to get a feel for it from the written accounts in *UltraRunning*. Wasatch has a reputation for nasty weather. Peter Gagarin says that the course is 3-4 hours slower than any of the others (except for Hardrock, which is in a class of its own) and demands as much from an ultrarunner as any course he can imagine; then he imagines a harder course which would consist of the first third of Wasatch, the middle third of Leadville and the final third of Pacific Crest with the final few miles of Western States thrown in along with the humidity of OD.

In addition to the hills, which add up to over 45,000 feet of combined elevation gain and loss, previous Wasatch runners have experienced high winds, oven-like heat, rain, fog, mud, sleet, hail, snow, fire, moved ribbons, and below-zero wind chill factors. The race application warns runners to beware of deer, elk, moose, porcupines, rattlesnakes, bears, mountain lions, sheep, sheepherders, blue heelers, and attack cats. Since 1980, 1015 athletes have started Wasatch and 599 finished, a 59% finishing rate, actually pretty good compared with the Leadville rate of 49%.

The Profile comments about Wasatch all follow the same theme. Denny Hagele of Palatine, Illinois, calls the race, "One tough mother from go to finish"; Todd Leigh of San Diego, California, says Wasatch is the "most difficult and challenging of all..." while Herb Tanimoto of Cool, California, notes it is "a course that never quits, never lets up."

I'm starting to get a feel for this event and it doesn't sound like a race for the timid or for the ill-prepared. While the ruggedness of the Wasatch Front is emphasized, those who have written about the race also mention the beauty of the mountains, of running through mile after mile of deep green pines gracing ridge after ridge. They talk about the crystalline air — so clear that you can see in any direction for 100 miles — and the lights of Salt Lake City, illuminated like jewels in the night.

Monday. 5 September. Bad news. This afternoon when I return home from work a note from my 17 year old son is waiting for me on the kitchen counter.

"Dad. I've gone to live with Mom. I'll be in touch. Steve."

A chill runs through my body, my knees weaken, and I slump to the floor. I'm taken completely by surprise, absolutely dumbfounded by this development. My ex-wife lives in Tampa, Florida, 600 miles away.

My 14 year-old-daughter is looking at me waiting to be driven to soccer practice.

"What's going on?" is all I can ask.

"Steve's unhappy. He's decided to go live with Mom."

"Yes, I know, but why?"

What a shock. Since my divorce ten years ago I have devoted my life to raising my kids. I have not remarried. My only social life has centered on running. I love my kids and have tried to bring stability to their lives. Over the years, people who know us have always complemented me on what a good job I was doing raising my children alone. Now this. I'm stunned. Suddenly, my thoughts are not of grand slamming. They are of my son.

Tuesday. 6 September. Harvey Hall has volunteered to be my crew/pacer again. I was resigned to doing Wasatch alone, but Harvey's presence will provide me with experienced support, especially after dark. The TV weather channel is predicting thunder storms in the Wasatch Mountains during the weekend.

The week before the race, I do no machine work and no long run, but I take my usual hilly one hour lunchtime runs, and I run ten miles every day of the Labor Day holiday weekend averaging 9 minute miles. My legs feel a little heavy, but strong, and I plan to do a lot of power walking during the race. My goal is to finish in less than 30 hours to win a turquoise buckle. I am prepared to give an all-out effort, keeping in mind the importance of finishing in order to complete the Grand Slam.

Salt Lake City lies at the base of the Wasatch Front, a 175 mile sweep of jagged mountains stretching from Provo in the south to Ogden in the north. On Wednesday, 7 September, Harv and I fly into the City of Saints on different flights that land within ten minutes of each other.

We rent a vehicle, go shopping for supplies, eat some seafood linguine for supper, and find our way up the Little Cottonwood Canyon Road to Cliff Lodge at Snowbird Resort. The granite used to construct the Church of Latter-day Saints Salt Lake Temple was quarried in Little Cottonwood Canyon. With its valet parking, Cliff Lodge is definitely more upscale than either of us is used to, but we adjust quickly. The idea is to spend our nights acclimatizing at 8,000 feet altitude, and the mountain view from our 9th floor room is terrific.

When I wake up on Thursday morning, my chest is sore, but I have no headache. Deciding to drive over to Midway to scout out the finish, we travel north to Big Cottonwood Canyon, head up to the small settlement of Brighton, then take a dirt road over Guardsman Pass and descend the eastern side of the Wasatch Mountains into the valley where lie Park City, Heber City, and Midway.

Once in Midway, I discover that I have forgotten the race map and the written instructions on how to reach the finish, but I remember enough so that after voyaging incorrectly in three different directions from the post office, we finally locate Stringtown Road then retrace the final three miles to the finish. Thoroughly exhausted by our foray into the gentle farmlands of Utah, we return to Brighton where we lunch at the General Store, site of the 73.7 mile aid station. One year, upon arriving at the aid station, a Wasatch runner locked himself in the cab of his pickup truck in the Brighton store parking lot and, despite the pleading of his friends, refused to come out. That was the end of his race.

Back at Cliff Lodge, a conference of vascular scientists is underway. These are brilliant people, heart and circulatory system experts, from all over the world — Japan, Germany, the U.K., the U.S. — and most of them are overweight and look like they haven't exercised in years. Many of them are smoking cigarettes and drinking booze like it's going out of style. Do they know something

I don't know? Do I know something they don't? I decide it's the latter.

I'm taking it easy, not running at all during these last few days before the race. For exercise I ride the Snowbird Tram to the top of 11,000 foot Hidden Peak and back down again. The high alpine meadows are covered with wildflowers. Formed 65 million years ago, these mountains are one of the most highly mineralized areas in the United States. Glaciation accounts for the many small lakes and extensive deposits of moraine materials characteristic of the Wasatch Front.

Friday, September 9. A beautiful sunny day in Utah. After spending the morning preparing my five drop bags, I eat lunch at an outdoor restaurant at Snowbird then drive into Salt Lake City, the Utah Zion, for the 4 PM pre-race briefing conducted at the Lake Terrace Pavilion in Sugarhouse Park. This briefing is even more low key than the one at Old Dominion. After weighing-in I have to ask for my race packet which contains two shirts - one long sleeved, one short sleeved — and my race number, 74.

A woman asks for my local phone number "for when you drop out." Insulted, I respond, "Madam, I have every intention of finishing this race."

John Grobben of Springville, Utah, directs the Wasatch Front 100. His speech takes about 15 minutes. Basically, he says drink a lot, tell us if you drop out, and good luck. Nothing about trail markings, and nobody asks. About a third of the runners are locals, so they know what to expect. Maybe the rest of us are brain dead. My excuse is that I'm busy taking photos of my Grand Slam heroes — Cindy, Burgess, El Burro. The anxiety level here is far lower than at Leadville or Western States — probably due to the lack of hoopla surrounding Wasatch.

An ESPN2 cameraman is interviewing Dixie Madsen and Rob Volkenand. At 57 and 63, they are the oldest female and male starters. Rob and Rick Gates are each going for their tenth Wasatch finish. Rick's best time is 25:55 in 1991. Rob is a member of the exclusive Royal Order of the Crimson Cheetah, comprised of those who have broken 24 hours at Wasatch. Since the race started in 1980, only 21 runners have qualified for the Crimson Cheetah belt buckle, not a single woman among them. The men's course record is 20:29:28, held by Dana Miller, while the women's mark is 24:34:54, set by Deborah Wagner in 1993 when she was 42.

As I chat with some of my cronies, the talk turns to injuries. Bob Solorio of San Francisco tells me that he tried the Slam in 1993 and got all the way to the 88th mile of Wasatch before dropping out with a badly sprained ankle. Larry Ochsendorf says that he ran Old Dominion with a painfully swollen achilles tendon and had a very sore calf muscle for the first 40 miles of Western States when both injuries miraculously vanished. Although this is Larry's first Wasatch 100, he seems calm and confident.

Not me. I'm in a daze. My readings about the difficulty of the course — the wild weather, the endless steep rocky climbs and descents — have left me with the impression that I am about to embark on the ultimate personal-growth wilderness adventure.

3 AM. Saturday. 10 September. Bewitching hour. The "black diamond" of trail 100s beckons. Harv and I are up. I'm bolting down orange juice, yogurt, and a cinnamon roll. I'll hold the Powerbar until we are on the road to East Layton, 20 miles north of Salt Lake City where the race starts.

A bus transports many runners to the start. Harv wants to drive. The directions provided by race management are explicit, so we set off on Interstate 15 and bear right on Highway 89. We are looking for a Key Bank and two Texaco stations for our next turn. It's 4:15 in the morning. The race starts at 5 AM. Somehow we miss our turn and wind up in South Weber, Utah.

"Harv, how did we miss two Texaco stations?" I'm keyed up; my jaws grind the Powerbar. Harv is wide awake; we're both leaning forward in anticipation of the race. My watch says 4:30. "Let's turn around and really keep our eyes open this time."

Returning along Highway 89, we somehow miss the turn again. "Shit, Harv, what's going on? Where the hell is the turn?"

Twisting around in the front seat to look out the back window I notice a recvee and another vehicle making right turns.

"That must be it, Harv. Let's turn around and follow those cars." 4:45 AM.

At last, we're on Valley View Drive then Fernwood Drive where lots of cars are parked. It's a residential neighborhood, a strange place for a trail race to start.

We park our rental car. Ten minutes to go. As I'm hurrying up Fernwood Drive strapping on my butt pack, someone stops his vehicle and yells at me.

"What's going on?"

"Damned if I know," I reply.

At 5 AM a gunshot in the fog evokes cheers and 145 trail runners start jogging in place until there is room to move forward. The initial 5.5 miles takes us through a scrub oak and salisbury brush landscape, starting at 5000 feet, to the top of "Chinscrapper" a ridge at 9170 feet. I've been curious about this climb, one of the more notorious ascents among the major trail 100s. The typical jockeying for position occurs with faster runners making suicidal attempts to go around slower runners. I'm guilty of this once or twice. By Horny Toad Junction, two miles into the race, everyone is spread out, comfortable with the pace, and the sense of urgency recedes, at least temporarily.

The climb turns out to be easier than Hope Pass except at the very top. "Chinscrapper" is a 30-yard scramble on hands and knees up a nearly vertical scree slope to the top of the ridge. I'm not going fast enough over the loose rocks to satisfy one of the female competitors who churns past kicking dust and pebbles in my face.

Peeking over the ridge crest, I'm stunned by a phenomenal view of the entire Salt Lake Valley bathed in dawn pastels. In the rush to keep moving I don't have time to soak in all the details of this spectacular panorama.

The narrow trail bears south on Rattlesnake Ridge. Frenzied runners are tearing along at breakneck pace trying to make up the time they think they have lost in the first five miles. With no place to pass or to step off the faint sheep trail to let the speed demons go by, I am forced to run faster than I should.

Suddenly, without warning, I find myself inverted in mid-air, landing sprawled out in a full length bellyflop with my outstretched hands hanging on to the edge of the trail. How in the world did that happen? My feet must have gotten tangled up. Other runners, hotfooting it past, observe me curiously. No one offers to help me up. The side of the mountain I am clinging to is so steep I'm afraid that if I let go I will toboggan all the way back down to Fernwood Drive.

It's either pull myself back onto the trail or lie here all day so I scramble up, brush the dirt off, ascertain that I'm not injured, and move on. Soon the Francis Peak Radar Domes come into view. Before reaching the Radar Domes the course connects with Francis Peak Road at Grobben's Corner, where a water point has been set up. After passing the Radar Domes, I'm momentarily confused at an unmarked road junction. Another runner advises me to keep to the right; then it's 2000 feet downhill in four miles to the road maintenance shed aid station.

Larry Ochsendorf, class of 1994, at Wasatch pre-race briefing.

by Robert Boeder

The descent makes my bowels rumble. Francis Peak Road is cut into the side of a steep incline, so I have to climb up a short cliff in order to find a private place where I can relieve myself. Crouching there with my shorts down, spying on the other runners as they trot past, I feel giddy in the morning air.

At 9 AM I arrive at the 14.6 mile check point to discover Harvey visiting with Nancy Hamilton, who is crewing for her husband, Rick. The Hamiltons organized the Catoctin 35 km trail event I ran in March. I didn't realize Rick was running Wasatch this year because they weren't at the pre-race briefing. I'm feeling expansive and finding Nancy there makes me euphoric. Her winning smile exudes energy.

"This is a great race, Harv. You'll have to do it next year," I yell exhuberantly. So far I'm having fun. Little do I know what awaits me.

More dirt road running for the next several miles. I'm asking myself, "Hey, where's the beef?"

Race volunteers have established an aid station at Charlie's Junction, the 16.9 mile point. After passing through the aid station, I'm running alone but with several other runners in sight in front of me. Suddenly, the road peters out. I can't find any trail markers. Other runners are milling around at a loss for where to go next. After a few minutes a runner catches up who shows us the way across some beaver ponds to a marked trail that appears freshly cut. Soon "the beef" appears: a steep climb traversing several streams, through a heavily forested area, and across a meadow.

I feel like I've been ambushed. This is tough. Reaching the Bountiful B Checkpoint at Mile 20, all of a sudden I'm hot and tired. After the aid station, a jeep trail takes me past some fragrant mountain mahogany, through more meadows, under a power line, up and down steep hills, to a camp site where the Sessions Lift-Off aid station (24.8 miles) has been set up.

I'm carrying three water bottles and consuming fluids at every opportunity, but it doesn't seem like enough. At Sessions Lift-Off, I fill all three bottles, drink a cup of Coke, and eat some melon before continuing south. The course follows the Great Western Trail through a wooded section of yellow quaking aspens and bright red sugar maples before climbing the aptly named Lung Sucker Hill to the Sessions Mountain ridge top at 9000 feet, the marathon point in the race.

Up here, the wind blasts me head on. Facing southwest, directly into the gale, I seem to be just running in place. Ducking my head so my cap isn't torn off, I twist my body to the left so my right shoulder is taking the brunt of the tornado. Progress is slow. I'm taking a pounding. Most of the trail is above the tree line, so there is no protection from the elements.

Eventually, an aid station appears 800 feet below me next to a road. The trail descends in a series of steep switchbacks. I cross Highway 65, the route the Mormons took into Salt Lake Valley nearly 150 years ago, and enter Big Mountain aid station. Situated in a large dirt parking lot, Big Mountain is a medical check point. I am 7 pounds under my starting weight, the most I have ever lost during an ultra.

My crewman is there to meet me.

"Harv, this course is meaner'n snot. It's tougher'n woodpecker's lips. Where are we?"

"It's the 36 mile point, Bob."

I'm shocked. It feels like I have run 50 miles. This is not going well. To relieve the tightness in my legs I squat down beside a vehicle in the only shade I can find. As I peel off the stinking, dusty shirt I have been wearing all morning, my body feels like it has been sand blasted. After wiping my arms, legs, face and neck with a wet towel, I put on a clean white shirt and a new hat.

"Put some ice in my water bottles when you fill them up, Harv." Before leaving, I place ice in my hat and take a mouthful. I feel partially rejuvenated, but the exhilaration of the early morning has worn off; it has been replaced by the grim knowledge that I'm in a real fight for survival here. The thought of quitting does not enter my mind, but when I started I had no idea Wasatch was going to be this difficult.

Runners are spread out along the course. Most of the time I am alone. The section following Big Mountain is well marked with white ribbons, so there is no problem following the jeep trail, but I feel lousy, like I'm going to throw up. Wasatch is famous for "eating its young" in the first 35 miles. I'm being devoured.

This is the worst I have ever felt during an ultra. The nausea and weight loss indicate I'm dehydrated. I need to consume fluids, but every time I drink anything it feels like I'm going to vomit. Normally, I favor downhills, but now the nausea increases on the descents. I feel fine on the uphills, so I find myself in the unusual position of looking forward to the climbs.

The area that I am traversing, between Bald Mountain and Pence Point, 41 miles into the race, has very poor footing. Loose rocks on the trail remind me of the Massanutten Mountain terrain at Old Dominion. I tell myself that if I survived Massanutten Mountain without breaking an ankle I won't get hurt here.

I catch up with another runner. As I pass him, we don't speak. This is odd. Normally, at least greetings are exchanged. Glancing at his face tells me the reason. He looks as bad as I feel. I'm not talking because we are negotiating Baugh Bearing Hill, a steep, treacherous downhill section full of loose rock. Descending this monstrosity safely requires all the concentration I can muster. In the valley ahead, power lines and the Alexander Springs 46 mile aid station come into view.

At Alexander Springs, I drink a Coke and carefully eat some saltine crackers hoping they will settle my stomach. Leaving the aid station, I'm feeling a little better and start to run along a grassy two track sheep path. This is the first running I have down in several hours and I'm pleased with myself. After 20 minutes of running I arrive at a bunch of ribbons indicating a sharp right turn. The trail passes through dense undergrowth. After climbing over a ridge, I join a dirt road. I can see a large highway in the distance. It must be I-80. The dirt road drops down to my left eventually zig-zagging to Parley's Creek. The trail follows the creek downstream where it turns left for the short climb to the Lambs Canyon aid station, the halfway point in the race. It's 7 PM. It has taken me 14 hours to run 50 miles, an all-time personal worst.

Upon weighing in I am given some bad news. I have lost an additional two pounds, so I'm nine pounds under my starting weight. Passing quickly through the aid station without eating anything or talking to anyone, I feel myself losing control. Harvey is supposed to be here to meet me. When I don't see him I break down in tears hiding my face in my hands so no one will see me. This emotional collapse is entirely involuntary. It just sweeps over me. I am embarrassed. I feel helpless, defeated.

Harv is waiting for me at the car park near the Interstate. The sound of traffic is unnerving. I am 52, Harv is 28. I'm like a big middle-aged baby standing there in front of him — miserable, bedraggled, tear-stained. To his great credit, Harv stays calm and focuses on keeping me in the race.

"What can I get for you, Bob?" he asks.

"I don't know," I reply. My dedication to finishing this race is evaporating.

"That's all right. We'll get you out of here in good shape. How about a banana?"

"I dont think I can keep anything down." I keep having fits of sobbing. After 350 miles, my Grand Slam dream has turned into a nightmare.

"Try some water."

"I feel sick." Why can't I get a grip on myself?

Eventually, after much patient prodding, Harv has refilled my bottles, I have eaten a banana and consumed a can of liquid food without any adverse effects. I have also managed to change into my cold weather night gear. Changing clothes involves standing naked in the road while Harv pulls off my gaiters, shoes, and socks and helps me put on running tights, clean socks, shoes, and the gaiters which aren't much use anymore because the stirrups have worn through.

My crying time is over. My sorrows are behind me. I feel emotionally drained but a lot better than when I arrived at Lambs Canyon. I have exchanged sunglasses for my normal glasses. Armed with two flashlights, I'm ready to go again.

Harv and I jog up the dirt road to the highway underpass. The fellow who was struggling at Baugh Bearing Hill is smiling and talking with his crew. We exchange the thumbs up sign. Harv stays with me for the two miles up Lambs Canyon Road to the Lambs Trailhead on our right.

The last thing he says is, "Just remember, Bob, you've got 20 hours to go 50 miles. Piece of cake."

Darkness is closing in. The trail crosses a stream then comes to a T-junction that isn't marked. Which way? Instinct tells me left. Twenty yards down the trail my intuition is rewarded by the appearance of a glow stick. The course ascends to the southwest, 1,400 feet in a mile and a half, to the crest of the ridge called Bare

Ass Pass, that separates Lambs and Millcreek Canyons. It's like climbing a staircase covered with loose rocks and boulders through the deepening shades of night.

Upon reaching the top, I'm jubilant, but the rejoicing is short lived because several paths branch out from the clearing and no glow stick marks the correct one. My intuition takes over again. This path heading to the right feels like the one I'm supposed to take. After a few minutes I find myself fighting through a clump of sharp-tipped scrub oak bushes. This can't be right.

Retracing my steps to the top of the pass, I choose another path which heads downhill. The glow sticks reappear and bliss envelopes me. I'm terrified of being lost. Catching up with two runners, the three of us reach the paved Millcreek Canyon Road. It's not marked. Which way now? Left or right? A woman sitting in a vehicle waiting for her runner tells us to go left, uphill, to the next aid station at Big Water.

My new companions, Steve and Jim, both from Utah, are good company - talkative, high spirited, full of jokes. Steve asks me if I know what to call a seagull flying over a bay.

"No, I sure don't."

"A bagel."

Most of this three mile road section is uphill, and I'm doing my best to powerwalk it. Traffic assails us. I assume it's crews traveling to and from Big Water. Some drivers dim their lights when approaching us. I have to shield my eyes from the ones who don't. Some slow down, others do not, forcing us onto the shoulder of the road alongside Millcreek. Sounds of laughter and partying come from several brightly lighted cabins. Facing the long cold night, I'm glad for the company of my two companions.

At the 60-mile point in the race, Big Water is a major aid station with lights, generators, tents and vehicles parked everywhere. Steve and Jim are welcomed by their crews. Harv and I follow our usual aid station routine, reloading bottles and serving up my liquid meal. I can never get the tops off these stupid cans by myself, so Harv does it for me. I wait impatiently while he fetches a cup of chicken soup. It's scalding hot. Carrying a water bottle and flashlight, my hands are full so I tell him to keep the soup.

It's after midnight when I finally exit the aid station. Up ahead I spot a familiar figure and quicken my pace until I join Rob "Ole

Goat" Volkenand. The trail is uphill, but unusually wide and smooth, like it has been swept clean with a broom. Rob says mountain bikers groom the trail.

I expect Rob to have a personality to match his nickname — crusty and rough around the edges — but I find him to be quite the opposite. He's a quiet, unassuming guy who doesn't seek publicity or accolades for his many years of being a top age-group trail ultrarunner. Apparently, the "Ole Goat" handle comes from Rob's stylish vandyke goatee. His demeanor, befitting someone who has trekked hundreds of solitary miles on mountain trails, resembles that of a zen master

Armin Wunder of Waldbronn, Germany, class of 1991, at Desolation Lake.

Running a long downhill together, we stay alert for a sharp left turn. After a half mile of uncertainty, we arrive at Blunder Fork and commence a two-mile uphill trek toward Desolation Lake aid station at the 65 mile point. Rob pulls ahead of me on this section.

At 9200 feet, Desolation Lake is set in a bowl-shaped depression. It's after midnight. A cold wind moans, and lightning crashes off the surrounding ridge tops. Several runners are huddled around the fire at the aid station. I reject this cold comfort and rejoin the trail which takes me to Red Lover's Ridge at 9900 feet.

The weather on top of this ridge is wilder than in any of the other 100 mile races. It's like a scene from the creation of the universe, with thunder, lightning, a raging wind, and punishing rain. Bent over double, I scuttle like a sand crab among the rocks searching for course markers. Totally alone in the dark, I feel a combination of euphoria at being so close to the elements and panic that I will blunder off the edge of a cliff.

The markers don't fail me. They lead to the relatively protected southwest side of the ridge where the trail becomes a rough road which I follow to Scott's Pass aid station. At 9900 feet and 70 miles into the race, Scott's Pass is a grim halt on a frozen peak swept by a howling cyclone. Inside a tent, runners warm themselves. Outside, a volunteer is shouting at me, listing all the food the aid station offers. It strikes me that this fellow is drunk and showing off in the middle of the night. Angered and exhausted, I yell back at him, "Keep your voice down, I'm not deaf," and turn to ask another volunteer for some chicken soup.

Declining the offer of a warm place in the tent, I leave Scott's Pass behind. Beginning a long road descent, I haven't gone more than 100 yards when suddenly the soup I have been drinking erupts from my throat. Strange. That's never happened before. I ate nothing else at the aid station and can't figure why the soup won't stay down.

I should be running this downhill, but my feet hurt so I'm doing my version of a power walk. The road takes me through a dark forest to the paved Guardsman Pass road at Sleepy Hollow Junction. After more descent I round Nancy's Corner and eventually arrive at Big Cottonwood Canyon Road, where the course bears left commencing a steep uphill hike to the aid station at Brighton General Store (73.7 miles).

Brighton is a small ski resort settlement named after William Brighton, who built a hotel here in 1874. Harv is waiting for me in the parking lot in front of the Store. We go inside and I weigh in — 3 pounds under my starting weight. Runners are sprawled all over the place, in sleeping bags and on chairs. Somebody's crew member offers me his seat.

"No, thanks, I never sit down during a race."

He looks at me like I have just told him I'm a man from Mars.

Originally, I wanted to reach Brighton at 4 AM which would give me a fighting chance to finish in under 30 hours. That time has slipped. It's close to 5 when Harv and I leave. Taking 24 hours to run 74 miles is not a stellar performance, but this is Wasatch and I'm in strictly a survival mode. My focus is on finishing.

Leaving the store, we follow the paved road for a short distance then join an uphill trail behind Brighton Lodge. The trail is full of huge boulders. I marvel that my quads are still strong enough to take the strain of climbing this torturous rockfall. Soon, I find myself on a very steep section, nearly as vertical as Chinscrapper, climbing literally on my hands and knees. It's pitch dark. Harv is somewhere behind me. My flashlight is clenched firmly in my mouth. It doesn't occur to me that anything is wrong until Harv yells,

"Hey, Bob, wait a minute. This can't be right. We've lost the course."

I wait motionless while Harvey casts his flashlight beam left and right. Some of the ribbons marking the trails to be traversed after dark have been tied to stones and branches close to the ground because that's where we direct our flashlights. After several minutes of searching, Harv locates a trail ribbon that has been half covered with dirt kicked up by passing runners. We missed a right turn at the base of the cliff I'm hanging onto. Reversing direction, I crawl back down to the trail.

Daybreak finds us milling around an open area covered with gravel. We followed the trail downhill from a ridge into a basin where the markings disappear. I'm growing increasingly tired, becoming confused, punchdrunk, losing track of details and the sequence of events. While I wander aimlessly, Harv circles around. Finally, he discovers trail ribbons to our left. The original ribbons marking this turn have vanished.

The next miles are a jumbled memory of trails, jeep roads, aspen groves, climbs and descents. The early morning energy surge I experienced at Western States isn't happening at Wasatch. My exhaustion is bone deep. Arriving at Pole Line Pass aid station (aka Old Goat Saloon), I enquire what the mileage is and am devastated when told that this is the 82 mile point.

"Eighty-two! It's mid-morning and I still have 18 miles to go! Have we crossed Catherine Pass yet?"

This question evokes mirth and merriment from the saloon keepers.

"You went over Catherine's Pass 5 miles back."

"That must have been during the night. I didn't even realize it." More jovial outbursts from the locals. At 10,480 feet, Catherine's Pass is the highest point on the course.

The race has become a death march. I'm in a funk. For the first time in 14 weeks, a sliver of doubt penetrates my mind. The nagging notion of quitting intrudes on my hitherto positive internal dialogue.

"Who cares if I finish? Who cares about the Grand Slam? This race is a downer. The course sucks. The volunteers are jerks. The race director is a sadist. This was a crappy idea from the beginning. I even have to pay for my own trophy. I feel like just sitting down by the side of the road and waiting for someone in a vehicle to come by and pick me up."

However, at this point the course is all trail. The grim reality is that, with few roads and fewer vehicles, this area is too remote for me just to collapse in a heap and abandon the race. Even if I decide to drop out, I have no alternative but to keep moving to the next aid station.

We come to a place called Rock Springs which consists of three horse troughs. If a horse was tied to one of them I would steal it and ride out of this wilderness never looking back. No such luck today. After Rock Springs the trail drops steeply, forcing me to run.

Sensing my ratty mood, Harvey has been quiet for the past few hours. Now he perks up.

"Hey, Bob, the downhillman is back doin' the California Runner shake shake boogie."

"Aw, shut up, Harv. Go back to sleep."

But running downhill restores some life to my legs. Prospects improve, and I'm feeling better when we pull into the Mill Canyon aid station (88 miles).

After Mill Canyon the course proceeds downhill on a dirt road; then we join what looks like a freshly cut trail through a grassy area which eventually crosses Cascade Springs Road. If I'm going to sit down and quit, this is the place, but it's noon and I have 5 hours to cover just over 10 miles.

"By God, Harv, I think we can do it," I shout.

Below the road lies Tooth Springs, a pleasant pond in a meadow. Continuing our descent for another mile we cross the Provo Deer Creek bottoms before meeting a dirt road which takes us into Cascade Springs (93 miles), the final weigh in and aid station.

Cascade Springs is accessible to vehicles and several crews are waiting for their runners. It's hot, so we pause to take off our jackets and roll up our long sleeves and the leggings of our tights. Filling my water bottles with ice, I put a handful in my cap to cool the blood vessels feeding my brain.

The course is all road from here to the finish. Just east of Cascade Springs is "The Wall," an amazingly steep 500 foot climb. After we crest "The Wall," the fertile green Heber Valley lies before us, with Midway and the finish line in the distance.

Although it's downhill and other runners are passing us, I decline Harvey's suggestion that we run it in.

"It's too hot, Harv. The prize money is the same for 70th place as it is for 80th. I don't want to risk cramps and dehydration from trying too hard at this point."

So we settle into a trudge. Next to the heat, the big problem at this point is the dust aroused by the constant traffic between Cascade Springs aid station and Midway. Sweating and covered with grime, Harvey and I resemble mudmen. We must look truly bedraggled because someone in a Jeep stops and hands us a can of Coke. As the Jeep drives away Harvey says, "Hey, that was Heikki Ingstrom. Whatta guy."

Finally, our dusty trek ends at the paved Stringtown Road.

"Two miles to go and feeling fine," I sing out.

Still walking, we reach Midway's Main Street. Glancing over my shoulder, I see a woman behind us; she is actually running, trying to catch me. My testosterone level rises to meet this final challenge. Bursting into overdrive, dashing past the Midway Gym and Post Office on Main Street, picking up speed around the left turn on 100 West Street and grinning broadly with arms outstretched to the heavens, I sweep under the Wasatch Front 100 Mile Endurance Run finish banner.

34:07:32. 85th place overall out of 110 finishers. Eleventh out of the 12 Grand Slammers of 1994. I finally beat Lee Schmidt, who finishes 32 minutes behind me.

Besides Lee and I, the other members of the class of '94 are Doug McKeever of Bellingham, Washington, Mark Bodamer from Ellensburg, Washington, Tom O'Connell of San Jose, California, Paul Akiyama and Burgess Harmer, both from Reno, Nevada, Cindi Grunt of Welches, Oregon, Terry Smith of Deadwood, South Dakota, Ken Burge from Cleveland, Ohio, Luther Thompson from Woodbury, Minnesota, and Larry Ochsendorf of Apple Valley, Minnesota.

The man who gave us the Coke, Heikki Ingstrom of Salt Lake City, wins the race in 21:42:13. Laura Vaughn of Tahoe City, California, is the women's winner in 23:55:34, thus becoming the first female member of the Royal Order of the Crimson Cheetah. Rob Volkenand and Rick Gates finish Wasatch for the tenth time and receive commemorative rings. Californian Louise Comar was the person who forced me to run the last quarter mile of the Wasatch Front 100. Thank you, Louise.

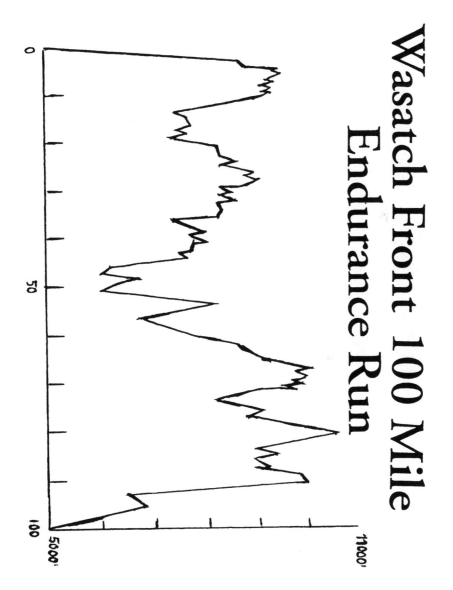

Wasatch Front 100 Mile Endurance Run

Class of 1989
(Front L-R):
Peyton, Thibeault, Klein, Adelman.
(Back L-R):
deSouza, Hooper, Ulrich, Mabry, Hardman, Eidenschink, Bassett.

by Janet Reffert/Action Photo

Class of 1994

(Kneelling L-R):
McKeever, Smith, Grunt, Akiyama, Ochsendorf.

(Standing L-R):
Boeder, Harmer, Thompson, Bodamer, Burge, O'Connell.
Not pictured — Schmidt

by Frank Ives

Chapter 6

History.

"The spirit of ultrarunning calls for a little anarchy and chaos to keep things interesting."

Fred Pilon.

What's the reward for finishing the Slam? The Eagle in Flight trophy engraved with the recipient's name and the names of the four races. Originally sculpted by H. Steven Anderson, of Salt Lake City, Utah, the ceramic Eagle in Flight is 14" high and sits on a 10" by 12" wooden base. The idea of having an eagle commemorate this achievement came from Wasatch Front 100 race director John Grobben who was inspired by a Biblical verse from the book of Isaiah, "They that wait upon the Lord...shall mount up with wings like eagles. They shall run and not be weary."

The trophy is the visible sign of success. The intangible payoff is membership in a special group of people — 40 as of the beginning of 1994 — who have accomplished this feat, plus a certain amount of admiration, status, and respect from one's peers in the small world of trail ultrarunning.

Before Tom Green became the first Grand Slammer, O.R. Petersen, of Vail, Colorado, had finished all four races, but not in the same year, and Rob Volkenand, of Bend, Oregon, had done four 100 milers in one summer, but not the big four. The accomplishments of these two pioneers impressed *UltraRunning* editor, Fred Pilon, who dreamed up the Slam, but when Fred tried it, he DNFed Old Dominion, the very first race. In the meantime, the

Grand Slam concept had been published in *UltraRunning* where Tom Green read about it and decided to take up the challenge.

Steve Baugh, the original director of the Wasatch Front 100, also read about the Slam in *UltraRunning* and suggested presenting a trophy to successful Slammers at the Wasatch awards ceremony. The first trophy was a sculpted male runner on a wood base. The Grand Slam concept has not been bureaucratized. No Grand Slam committee exists. All decisions affecting the Grand Slam are made by the Wasatch Front race committee on an ad hoc basis.

Between 1986 and 1993, 40 trail runners — 33 men and 7 women — completed the Grand Slam. Five people have done it more than once. Burgess Harmer of Reno, Nevada, is the Grand Slam Gorilla with four "Eagle in Flight" trophies. The oldest Grand Slammer, Helen Klein, from Rancho Cordova, California, was 66 in her year, 1989, also the first year for female finishers; Suzi Thibeault of Colfax, California, was the first woman to complete the Grand Slam followed closely by Helen, Lou Peyton of Little Rock, Arkansas, and Marge Adelman, of Denver, Colorado. Suzi suggested to John Grobben that perhaps the male-runner statue was not a suitable prize for female Slammers, so in 1989 the award was changed to the Eagle In Flight trophy.

The oldest men, Ed Williams of Cape Girardeau, Missouri, and Hal Winton, from Harbor City, California, were 61 in their GS years, 1990 and 1992, respectively. The youngest male, Armin Wunder of Waldbronn, Germany, was 23 in 1991 when he Slammed. Armin and Martyn Greaves of Pulborough, England, who completed all four races in 1988, are the only non-U.S. Slammers. The youngest woman, Kitty Williams Fisher, of Tucson, Arizona, was 32 in 1990 when she finished all four along with her dad, Ed Williams.

The Williams' are the only family four-race finishers and Kitty is the only Grand Slammer to retire from the sport following completion of the Slam. The most GSers in one year were 13 in 1992; the fewest was one, in 1986, the first year. California is the most popular home state with 12 Grand Slammers; the most prevalent age group is the 40's, with 19 runners. Before 1994, six men in their 50's had finished all four races. Tom Green was the only East Coast runner to complete the Slam until I made it and became the seventh successful GS athlete in his 50's.

Comparisons of ultra running performances are difficult to make because of differences in weather and trail conditions from year to year, but based on comparative times and overall placing, the top three Grand Slam achievements among the men belong to Marshall Ulrich of Fort Morgan, Colorado, in 1989 and Steve Mahieu of Albuquerque, New Mexico, and Joe Schlereth from Fresno, California,in 1991.

Steve Mahieu, class of 1991. One of the fastest Grand Slammers.

UltraRunning, Vol 11, No. 8, Jan — Feb 1992

What are the qualities required to complete the Grand Slam? In a 1987 *UltraRunning* article, Trishul Cherns noted, "The top trail runners must have the lungs of a miler, the footwork of a mountain goat, the balance of an acrobat, the strength of a marathon runner, and the endurance and patience of a 24-hour racer."

What motivates trail ultra runners? After finishing 12th at the 1994 Leadville 100, John Demorest tried to answer that question, "The answer lies at a profound emotional level, is extremely complex, resonating to all levels of our lives....There are several aspects: the need for challenges, proving myself through competition, getting in shape, conquering a seemingly impossible goal, the self-esteem that comes after its completion, my love for running in the wilderness, and the joy in performing in an environment like Leadville that brings out the best in human nature."

Multiple Western States women's winner, Bjorg Austrheim-Smith, waxes enthusiastic about the joys of running. "I absolutely adore running. I love trail running because it is so gorgeous. I would love to share this experience with other people. For me, it is a therapy and it frees me, and I would like other people to get that same feeling. When I just see them sitting....getting grumpy.... and not communicating with each other....they are unhappy. Life is entirely too short not to enjoy yourself. Look at what we are surrounded by, it is outstanding! And we should live in harmony with it, and go out and enjoy it, then come back and draw from it."

Running is therapeutic for me too. When I'm feeling depressed, nothing beats a 20-mile run to start the healing. The cathartic ingredient in extreme exercise reflects the spirit which surrounds ultrarunning. The discipline required to train for and run long distances creates a form of transcendence providing an escape from the ordinariness of life.

John Demorest acknowledges the mystical aspect of the sport: "These runs serve as an annual spiritual dance with the mountains that renews my life and sets the world straight; kind of a sacrifice of the body to renew the spirit."

No single statement explains why people put in all the effort required to run ultras, but Boston Marathon legend Johnny Kelley comes closest: "I'm afraid to stop. I don't want to give it up. If I drop dead from running, so what?" That's the spirit. That's what we want. That's a real runner talking.

Johnny Kelley ran 60 Boston marathons, but multi-day races have been run for centuries and ultramarathon length road races have long been a staple of the European, Australian, and South African sports scenes. In the 1920's, trans-continental races were popular in the United States, but the fad died out. In the 1950's, an African American, Ted Corbitt, pioneered modern ultrarunning. Ted competed on roads and the track, but not on trails.

Competitive long distance trail running was invented in 1974 by a 27 year old High Sierra woodcutter, Gordy Ainsleigh, when Gordy decided to enter the Tevis Cup horse race on the Western States Trail without a mount. Although advertised as a 100 mile race, the Tevis Cup course was closer to 86 miles long, but this takes nothing away from Gordy's achievement in completing the distance in 23:42. Two years later, Gordy's pal, Ken "Cowman" Shirk, another hippy/backwoods/cowboy type — who runs wearing a fur headpiece with antlers — duplicated Gordy's feat.

In 1979, Pat and Wayne Botts brought endurance trail running to the East Coast by organizing the Old Dominion 100 Mile Endurance Run. The sport emerged nationally in the 1980's. Most 100-mile trail runners are men in their 30s and 40s, though, the number of women entering trail races is growing, especially on the west coast.

What kind of people run 100-mile trail races? While the forerunners of the sport were certified eccentrics, a significant number of the elite competitors in the mid 1990's, including Western States winners Tim Twietmeyer of Auburn, California, and Tom Johnson, from Loomis, California, are engineers. They take pains in planning every aspect of their trail races down to the minutest detail.

But these athletes aren't devoted to problem solving for its own sake. It's more complicated than that. Trail runners are also romantics. As Kent Holder says, "Ultrarunners are dreamers. It all starts with an idea. The idea becomes a goal. When the goal is finally achieved, dreams come true."

Many ultra runners are antiauthoritarian, antibureaucratic - people who don't fit in. They are the hardcore survivors of the running boom of the 80's, dedicated to swimming against the tide, or, in this case, to running against the wind. They aren't quitters. They aren't saints. And, surprisingly, most of them are not loners.

Generally, people relate best to those with whom they have shared hardship. This sharing is one reason ultrarunning is such an intensely communal sport and why American trail ultrarunners form such a closeknit community. During a race and in the days and weeks leading up to an event, ultrarunners lean heavily on each other and on their loved ones for support. The shared effort forms a strong attachment between runners during a race. As they run or walk, they encourage each other, often recounting the stories of their lives down to the most intimate details.

Why do women do well in ultras? Ann Trason sees three elements in ultramarathoning: the physical, which is basically a matter of raw strength; the mental, which involves patience, control and tactics; and endurance, the ability to keep moving through exhaustion and adversity. Only the physical is gender-specific. Female ultrarunners have mastered the mental and endurance aspects. When they have as much talent, work as hard, and train on trails as much as Ann does, they can match the best men in strength.

Many male runners don't like to be beaten by a woman. Ann specializes in running hard at the end of a 100-mile race, picking off runner after runner (all men) in the final miles. They hate it but there is nothing they can do about it.

Ann is the only U.S. athlete who makes any money running long distances. She has a contract with Nike. She is the women's world record holder at 50 miles, 100 miles, and 100 kilometers and is equally adept on roads, track, and trails. It's wonderful that one from our obscure midst has made it into the high echelons of sport, the thin air where Michael Jordan resides. Of course, Ann doesn't make anywhere near what Jordan earns in a year, but at least she is recognized as a top athletic performer.

One advantage men enjoy over women in ultras is not having to worry about a period beginning at the 80 mile point of the race or at 3 AM on a trail in the middle of nowhere. Of course, women who are post-menopausal don't have to worry about this either. Along with their usual race preparation, many veteran lady ultramarathoners place Tampons alongside the energy bars in their drop bags and fanny packs.

Ultrarunning is about understanding one's own mind, body, and emotions. As Ann Trason, says,"...you really have to be in tune with yourself. You go through a whole lifetime of experience in one day. You go through every emotion."

The fascinating thing is that the emotions are as exaggerated as the physical stress one undergoes during a long race. The happy feelings are euphoric, the sadness produces fits of weeping, the anger can lead to ugly scenes of enraged runners shouting at their crews if they are not quick enough with a drink or a clean t-shirt. But all is forgiven and forgotten within the next 5 miles.

Most ultrarunners resist any psychoanalysis. Competitive, but good natured and relaxed about it they will race anyone at any distance from 100 yards to 100 miles. They don't take it personally if they lose and they won't rub it in if they win.

Anyone who has faced the dark hole of a DNF in the wee hours of the morning at the bottom of Veach Gap at Old Dominion will tell you that the important thing about a 100-mile race is finishing. Placement in the order of finish matters, but it is definitely secondary to completing the distance.

Ultrarunners have the reputation of being lunatics, but, in fact, in order to withstand the stresses of running 100 miles, a person must be emotionally stable and have his head screwed on tight.

"Conquer thyself" seems the most appropriate motto for ultrarunners. O.R. Petersen, wrote, "Our task is to enjoy the wilderness experience, suffer whatever pain and fatigue it may require, wrestle with our own personal demons, and if successful in defeating those demons, we reach the finish line."

Of course, death is the ultimate finish line. The Western States Participant's Guide warned me that running 100 miles qualifies as a veritable dance with death. Is the risk worth taking? Am I challenging the limits of human endurance, pushing myself to the extreme edge of human performance?

That's not the way I look at it. For me, running ultras has more to do with developing a healthy approach to life, combining good nutrition and intense training with a positive attitude and religious faith and it all works. I'm in great physical shape. I have no aches or pains. My muscles feel loose, and my joints are flexible. I don't consider myself remarkable, but some individuals in this sport are daring to go where few have ventured before.

As of 1994, the oldest man and woman to finish the Western States 100, Ed Fishman, of Honolulu, Hawaii, and Helen Klein, were 69. These runners are certainly extending the limits of human performance. As more people in our society live longer, these pathfinders of ultrarunning are teaching us what the human mind and body can accomplish. It's more than anyone dreamed.

Epilogue

"Finally, be strong in the Lord and in the strength of his power."

Ephesians, chap. 6, v. 10.

In every triumph there is loss. My son returned home after a month. In retrospect, I believe the self-absorption required to finish the Grand Slam blinded me to signs that he was feeling neglected.

To paraphrase Hunter S. Thompson, we live in strange times, and maybe runners are right, maybe physical fitness really is the last refuge of the liberal instinct. Nothing else has worked, and the ability to run 100 miles on trails might be a very handy skill to have for the coming ordeal of the 21st century.

The Wasatch Front 100 Miler ends in a town called Midway, but for me it marks the end of a quest, my pursuit of the Eagle in Flight trophy, and the culmination of 118 hours and 29 minutes of Grand Slam summer 1994 trail running.

After all the travail and stress,
The mortal struggle and the mortal fear,
They tumbled up at dawn,
Sleepy and cursing,
To see before them there,
Neither the forest nor another pass to climb,
But, thin in the distance, thin but dead ahead,
The line of unimaginable dreams.
The finish.

Grand Slammers
1986 — 1994

1986
Tom Green, MD (35)

1987
John Bandur, WA (49)
Herb Tanimoto, CA (39)

1988
Wendell Robison, WY (36)
Martyn Greaves, GB (29
Dennis Hagele, IL (44)

1989
Marshall Ulrich, CO (38)
Gordon Hardman, CO (38)
Chuck Eidenschink, OR (36)
Nick Bassett, CA (44)
Ferdinand deSouza, UT (36)
Suzi Thibeault, CA (42)
Max Hooper, AR (42)
Larry Mabry, AR (42)
Helen Klein, CA (66)
Lou Peyton, AR (45)
Marge Adelman, CO (39)

1990
Richard Gates, UT (33)
Burgess Harmer, NV (48)
Dick Collins, CA (57)
Roy Haley, TX (54)
Kitty Williams, TX (32)
Ed Williams, MO (61)

1991
Joe Schlereth, CA (41)
Steve Mahieu, NM (44)
Wendell Robison, WY (39)
Roy Haley, TX (55)

Burgess Harmer, NV (49)
Nick Klaich, NV (46)
Armin Wunder, GER (23)
Linda Elam, CA (45)

1992
Joe Schlereth, CA (42)
Rick Gates, UT (35)
Burgess Harmer, NV (50)
Hal Winton, CA (61)
Floyd Whiting, NV (51)
Lee Schmidt, CA (53) "El Burro"
Chris Cole, CA (29)
Todd Leigh, CA (50)
William Watson, SD (46)
Gary Wright, WA (41)
Fred Jorgensen, CO (44)
Frank Ingalls, IN (47) "Jim"
Fred Reimer, UT (44)

1993
Luther Thompson, MN (49)
Barbara Ann Miller, CA (48)

1994
Terry Smith, SD (40)
Larry Ochsendorf, MN (49)
Luther Thompson, MN (50)
Tom O'Connell, CA (43)
Cindie Grunt, OR (44)
Burgess Harmer, NV (52)
Mark Bodamer, WA (36)
Ken Burge, OH, (44)
Doug McKeever, WA (46)
Paul Akiyama, NV (50)
Bob Boeder, NC (52)
Lee Schmidt, CA (55)

Made in the USA
Middletown, DE
04 August 2020